DANISH YEARBOOK
OF
PHILOSOPHY

VOLUME 42

DANISH YEARBOOK OF PHILOSOPHY

VOLUME 42
2007

MUSEUM TUSCULANUM PRESS
UNIVERSITY OF COPENHAGEN 2008

Published for
Dansk Filosofisk Selskab
in cooperation with
the Philosophical Societies of Aarhus and Odense
and with financial support from
the Danish Research Council for the Humanities

*

EDITORIAL BOARD:

FINN COLLIN
University of Copenhagen
Chairman

JØRGEN HUGGLER
Danish University of Education

UFFE JUUL JENSEN
University of Aarhus

STIG ANDUR PEDERSEN
Roskilde University Centre

ERICH KLAWONN
Odense University

HANS SIGGAARD JENSEN
Copenhagen Business School

MOGENS PAHUUS
Aalborg University

LARS GUNDERSEN
University of Aarhus

*

Articles for consideration and all editorial communications should be sent in three copies to:
Danish Yearbook of Philosophy
University of Copenhagen, Department of Philosophy
Njalsgade 80, DK 2300 Copenhagen S, Denmark

Business communications, including subscriptions and orders for reprints, should
be addressed to the publishers:
MUSEUM TUSCULANUM PRESS
Njalsgade 126
DK 2300 Copenhagen S
Denmark

*

© 2008 DANISH YEARBOOK OF PHILOSOPHY
COPENHAGEN, DENMARK
PRINTED IN DENMARK
BY SPECIAL-TRYKKERIET VIBORG A-S

ISBN 978 87 635 0980 0
ISSN 0070-2749

CONTENTS

Andrew Feenberg: *Between Reason and Experience* 7-32

Kaj Børge Hansen: *Remarks on Wittgenstein's Philosophy: Private Language and Meaning* 33-73

Christian Beenfeldt: *Ungrounded Semantics: Searle's Chinese Room Thought Experiment, the Failure of Meta- and Subsystemic Understanding, and Some Thoughts about Thought-Experiments* 75-96

Søren Riis: *Genealogies of Modern Technology* 97-109

Esben Nedenskov Petersen: *Skepticism and Transcendental Arguments from Semantic Externalism* 111-122

BETWEEN REASON AND EXPERIENCE

ANDREW FEENBERG

Simon Fraser University

Introduction

Everyday experience has a teleological character that ancient science raised to the level of an ontological principle. In modern times the new mechanistic concept of nature shattered the harmony between experience and scientific rationality (Whitehead, 2004: 30-31). The world split into two incommensurable spheres, a rational but meaningless nature and a human environment still rich in meaning but without rational foundation. In the centuries since the scientific revolution no persuasive way has been found to validate experience or to reunite the worlds despite the repeated attempts of philosophers from Hegel to Heidegger. This is not just a theoretical problem. Experience teaches caution and respect for people and things. Experience brings recognition that the Other has its own powers, limits and goals. Once the lessons of experience no longer shape technical advance it is guided exclusively by the pursuit of wealth and power. The outcome calls into question the viability of modernity. The genocidal 20th century is now followed by a new century of environmental crisis.

Technology stands at the crossroads of all these developments. It is both an application of scientific-technical rationality and the background of the world of experience. Communication between the two realms ought to be possible around technical problems if nowhere else. Philosophy of technology thus has a unique vantage point from which to consider the modern dilemma. This vantage point has been occupied fruitfully by Heidegger, whose concept of world is deeply implicated in his notion of technical practice. Yet Heidegger himself failed to draw out the most important implications of this coincidence. In Marcuse a more socially concrete formulation of a similar approach opens the way to a solution which I will sketch in the conclusion of this paper.[1] Accordingly the paper is divided into three main parts, a first part on the relation of technique and world in Heidegger, a second part carrying the story further in Marcuse's Marxist reformulation of the Heideggerian approach, and a third part in which the concepts of technique and world are reconsidered in relation to environmental crisis.

The philosophical issue concerns the relation of norms derived from concrete experience to rationalized technical practice. The expulsion of teleology from scientific-technical rationality stripped it of most normative elements. So long as ethical and aesthetic principles remain external to technique they appear to intrude impotently on a self-sufficient domain with its own laws and logic of development. Thus nothing is more urgent today than rooting these principles in the structure of technical disciplines as restraints on the deployment of their overwhelming destructive power. Can this be accomplished in a progressive framework? Can normativity be restored within the technical realm without regressive re-enchantment of nature or general impoverishment? These are the questions to which this paper is addressed, not with final answers in hand but programmatically, in the hope of suggesting a new approach.

Technique and World in Heidegger

The place to begin is Heidegger's ontological account of experience, which he calls "worldhood" in an attempt to avoid any hint of subjectivism. Worlds emerge in the human encounter with reality, but that encounter cannot be understood in causal terms because on those terms no world appears but only isolated stimuli and response. "World" must be understood instead as the existential enactment of meaning, not the object of perception. But despite the rejection of a causal account, Heidegger describes the encounter with world in more or less passive terms as a revealing, a disclosure, an opening, not a construction. His language struggles to evoke this enactment, which is taken for granted and indeed must be taken for granted, for everyday life to go on.

These are familiar aspects of Heidegger's early thought, but it seems to me that insufficient attention has been paid the nature of the enactment in which worlds emerge. This relative neglect is I believe due to the entwinement of Heidegger's argument from the very beginning with a phenomenological concept of the technical that challenges philosophy to leave its ivory tower and engage with concrete social reality. His work promises a new basis for understanding human life through a radical reevaluation of the structure and relevance of everyday experience in its technical aspect.

That Heidegger himself failed to fulfill this promise, that his attempts to concretize philosophy are still excessively abstract, that his early vision of the technical later degenerated into a global critique has authorized much evasion and obscurity. And where philosophers attempt to fulfill the promise of

Heidegger's technical turn, they all too often attribute to him intentions that he no doubt should have entertained rather than recognizing the limitations of his actual position. Such appropriation of Heidegger's philosophy begins with the early writings of his student, Herbert Marcuse. I will return to this connection in the second part of this paper.

The infamous Rectoral Address contains an intriguing ambiguity relevant to my argument. The subject of the Address is "Wissenschaft" and its place in the university. In 1933 Heidegger imagined that he could realize his own philosophy through collaboration with the Nazi regime. He hoped to stimulate a reform of the university that would bring its disciplines into a renewed version of the original "Greek" relationship to the world. That relationship he described as one of fearless questioning of reality combined with submission to "fate." Characteristically, he failed to provide any concrete guidelines for accomplishing this in modern Germany. But even while remaining at an ineffectually high level of abstraction, his argument hints at interesting possibilities.

Heidegger quotes a saying attributed to Prometheus that, he claims, "expresses the essence of knowledge." The text reads "techne d'anangkes asthenestera makro," translated as "But knowledge is far less powerful than necessity" (Heidegger, 1993a:31). Note that Heidegger translates "techne" as "knowledge" and thus apparently confounds the know-how of practical making (techne) with the Wissenschaften (epistemai) of university professors. And he insists! In the following paragraphs he rejects the familiar notion that the Greeks idealized disinterested contemplation and writes instead that for them

> "theory" does not happen for its own sake; it happens only as a result of the passion to remain close to what is as such and to be beset by it. On the other hand, however, the Greeks struggled to understand and carry out this contemplative questioning as a – indeed as *the* – highest mode of man's *energeia,* of man's "being at work." It was not their wish to bring practice into line with theory, but the other way around: to understand theory as the supreme realization of genuine practice (Heidegger, 1993a:31-32).

This obscure formulation must have puzzled his audience. Only his own students would have understood what Heidegger meant by these references to techne and energeia and this unconventional explanation of Greek science as dependent on practice. In his contemporary lectures he explains that the metaphysical concept of energeia derives from labor aiming at an essential accomplishment. Energeia is actuality in the sense of the realizing of the work. The fullest actuality of man is the realization of his capacities, his "dynamis," in "being at work" in the practice of a techne. He argues that it is out of this practice that the sciences emerged at the origins of Greek thought when technical engagement with beings evolved into wonder. Heidegger writes:

> it is clear that this perceiving of beings in their unconcealedness is not a mere gaping, that wonder is carried out rather in a procedure against beings, but in such a way that these themselves precisely show themselves. For that is what *techne* means: to grasp beings as emerging out of themselves in the way they show themselves, in their outward look, *eidos*, idea, and, in accord with this, to care for beings themselves and to let them grow, i.e., to order oneself within beings as a whole through productions and institutions (Heidegger 1994, 155).

In sum, Heidegger appears to be saying that scientific knowledge of the nature of things is not essentially contemplative but grows out of practical craft knowledge.[2] But knowing implies more than making. In knowing, the meaning of what is becomes explicit as idea, essence, and is grasped, Heidegger assures us, in wonder. This respectful attitude lies at the foundation of the sciences and must be recaptured for the university to return to its rightful role in society.

The identification of knowledge and techne is familiar from pragmatism but Heidegger does not reduce truth to consequences. Knowledge is rooted in instrumental activity in the broadest sense but not in that aspect of it that serves mastery of the environment. Technical power worries Heidegger more and more, but at least until the mid 1930s, the *form* of technical practice has a very broad significance for his philosophy. It is the fact that instrumental activity brings forth something prefigured in an image, an eidos, that interests him. In his course on Aristotle's *Metaphysics* he offers such an account of techne, explaining the teleological conception of being as a generalization from craft practice. Everything thus has an essence that prefigures it and so can be known (Heidegger, 1994: 76-77).

Essences, as the guiding principles of techne, are founded in elemental practical coping with the world and appear in the first instance in the structuring of technical practice around right and wrong ways of transforming matter. The essence, as peras and telos, limit and goal, is immanent in the practice of making which responds to the specific privation the materials suffer in their formless condition at the outset of the work. Essences are not in the first instance in the mind as ideas, but in the hands as gestures and in the materials as an obscure striving fulfilled in the finished work. The logic of techne is thus privation and fulfillment.

This is the background to Heidegger's explanation of everyday use in *Being and Time*. There he argues that using is not the implementation of a pre-existing plan but possesses "its own kind of sight." This sight, "Umsicht," identifies significances, meanings, not intellectually but in action. Meaning is thus manifest in experience prior to its propositional articulation, a fundamental phenomenological insight.

There is, however, a danger associated with techne that Heidegger emphasized increasingly as his work matured. Techne imposes limitation on the formlessness of the materials. But in this there is a risk of arbitrariness, of violently imposing a merely subjective order on things rather than disclosing them in their truth. This notion of arbitrariness can be interpreted in two different ways. First, the arbitrary may manifest itself as error, deviation from the essential pattern at which production should aim. Second, culture itself may be conceived as arbitrary. Affirming arbitrariness in this second sense involves relativizing any and all meanings. Heidegger's Greeks were aware only of the first form of arbitrariness. The later Heidegger argued that modernity is based on the second form which now prevails as the technological revealing.

In the technological revealing, no essences are uncovered. The place of meaning is now taken by the plan and so reduced to human intentions. This may be described as hubristic although as the technological system gathers momentum it humbles its human creators by incorporating them into its system. This critique of technology was not explicit in Heidegger's writings until the mid 1930s, but he assumed its main points already.

Heidegger's "reform" of the university was intended to block such arbitrariness by tying scholarship to the limits of a techne. At that time, Heidegger considered statesmen to belong to a superior order of producers.[3] The techne in question was thus the formation of the Nazi state. The university was to maintain its autonomy precisely through subordinating its understanding of the world to the intrinsic necessities and limits of the national restoration brought about by Hitler. In Heidegger's own mind, this was quite distinct from politicizing Wissenschaft by infusing it with political propaganda.

Beyond Heidegger's personal error, what are the strengths and weaknesses of this conception? Heidegger is most convincing in arguing that knowledge is ultimately rooted in the enactment of meanings in everyday practice. This argument against the neutrality and autonomy of knowledge is echoed in contemporary epistemology and sociology. The notion that meanings are to be found not primarily in the mind as conceptual maps but in action as the guiding principles of practical behavior is especially suggestive.[4]

But there is a puzzling risk of self-referential contradiction in Heidegger's approach. Only in the age of technology is it possible to adopt a synoptic view of the history of being such as Heidegger's. He holds that like all previous humans, we moderns live in a realm of meaning that is given to us through a tradition as access to a world. According to this tradition, there is a world "in itself" that can be known in its truth scientifically, but that is grasped in one or another arbitrary way in a collective subjectivity, a culture. But this view merely recapitulates a technological understanding of being as raw materials subject to a plan. In sum, we can articulate a general theory of the local origin of culture, a "history of being," because we are situated in a culture that understands all meanings as reducible to the subject. Heidegger must have been aware of the reflexive paradox implicit in his position.[5] He attempted to overcome the paradox in quasi-Hegelian terms, the "owl of Minerva" rising at the dusk of modernity. A "new beginning" would place Germany in touch with a new order of meaning beyond the reach of the relativizing consciousness that enables Heidegger to think the limitation of modernity as a specific culture.

What could the new sources of meaning be? Surely not the arrogant strutting of those "Aryan worthies" intoxicated by newspapers and beer whom Nietzsche had already denounced fifty years before (Nietzsche, 1956, pp. 294-295)! Heidegger's essentially dogmatic claim that a new era had begun is untenable, easily refuted by the very modern thought he hoped to transcend. The breakdown of this whole construction led the later Heidegger to a new position based on poetic thinking. But that new position cancels the original reformist intent of his early philosophy. The call for a "free relation" to technology may not imply total resignation, but it certainly is not a program of technological reform.

Marcuse, Lukács, Heidegger

I want to turn now to a further consideration of that reformist intent and Marcuse's relation to it. The reason I focus on Marcuse is not merely biographical. What concerns me is the prevalence of contemporary Heidegger scholarship that struggles heroically with the texts of the master in the interests of some sort of left wing politics. This is no doubt a minority view, but it has interesting advocates. The influence of Derrida and Foucault is important in this connection, as is the plausible analogy between Heideggerian Gelassenheit and some sort of environmental philosophy (Schürmann, 1990; Foltz, 1995). Environmentalist, anarchist, and postmodern interpretations are offered on this basis.

But the improbability of all these interpretations is clear from Heidegger's last interview in which he dismissed democracy and praised the Nazi revolution which, he still claimed, confronted the real problems but in too limited a manner to solve them (Heidegger, 1993a: 104, 111). If there is something of value in Heidegger, as I believe there is, it can only be extracted by sacrificing fidelity to his doctrine. The way to get at this worthwhile contribution is critically, not just exegetically.

This is precisely what Marcuse did during his years as Heidegger's assistant. To some extent the influence of Heidegger continued in Marcuse's later thought as well. In what follows I will try to outline the transformation Heidegger's argument underwent in Marcuse's writings. This cannot be a straightforward procedure since Marcuse reacted so strongly against Heidegger that he substituted similar ideas from other sources for those of his teacher. Heidegger's influence survives as a kind of archaeological stratum underneath these later sources, only occasionally emerging into view.

What was it in *Being and Time* that so excited Marcuse as to inspire him to return to the university as Heidegger's student? He later explained that it was the promise of a "concrete" philosophy (Olafson, 2007: 116). This promise accompanied the rebellion against scientism which took an original turn in the early 20th century. Instead of romantic protest against reason in the name of passion, existential ontologists developed an analytic of first person experience which they interpreted as the foundation of the abstractions in which science consists. For many philosophers, phenomenology was the essential methodological innovation that enabled the turn to a concrete ontology. It was this turn that attracted Marcuse.

What was unusual about Marcuse's situation was his strong political sympathies. He was a revolutionary socialist bereft of party and hope after the failure of the German revolution in 1919. There were many different diagnoses of the sickness of German socialism, but the one that appealed to Marcuse was laid out most persuasively in 1923 in Georg Lukács's famous book, *History and Class Consciousness*. There Lukács introduced the concept of reification to broaden Marx's original critique of market rationality into a more radical critique of scientific-technical rationality as the dominant cultural form in modern capitalist society. He notes the similarity between scientific knowledge and the laws of the market Marx criticized. The market is a "second nature" with laws as pitiless and mathematically precise as those of the cosmos. Lukács writes, "What is important is to recognize clearly that all human relations (viewed as the objects of social activity) assume increasingly the objective forms of the abstract elements of the conceptual systems of natural science and of the abstract substrata of the laws of nature" (Lukács, 1971: 131).

Like the worker confronted by the machine, the agent in a market society can only manipulate these laws to advantage, not change them. "Man...is a mechanical part incorporated into a mechanical system. He finds it already preexisting and self-sufficient, it functions independently of him and he has to conform to its laws whether he likes it or not" (Lukács, 1971: 89).

We are not far here from Heidegger's later critique of technology as a universal mode of thought and action in modernity. But unlike Heidegger Lukács envisaged a politics of dereification. As a Marxist he argued that the human reality underlying the reified forms can reassert itself and transform the society (Feenberg, 2005: chap. 4). But reification distorts and obscures the process character of social reality in both theory and practice. Fundamental change requires a shift in perspective.[6]

Lukácsian reification involves an objectivistic misunderstanding of the social world as composed of law-governed things subject to theoretical representation and technical manipulation, precisely the worldview against which Heidegger and Marcuse also protested in their early work. Reading Heidegger, Marcuse discovered a path to an existential formulation of the Lukácsian argument in terms of the concept of authentic action, freed from the social democrats' passive conformity to economic law. This formulation could then be turned to account in addressing the problem of revolutionary consciousness for which the social democrats had neither solution nor, any longer, even concern. Accordingly, Marcuse joined a vaguely Heideggerian conception of individual decision with Marxist social theory. Once the decisive action of the authentic individual is treated in class terms as a collective enterprise, it provides an original account of the revolution as a transforming practice capable of dereifying society and remaking it anew.[7]

The early emphasis on the existential crisis of the individual continued throughout Marcuse's career although in his later work the references to both Heidegger and the proletariat were dropped. The important new element in Marcuse's thought that can traced to other aspects of Heidegger's influence is the critique of technology, especially in Marcuse's 1964 book *One-Dimensional Man*. With rare exceptions, the extent and nature of this influence has been consistently underestimated or misunderstood by both Marcuse's admirers and critics.

Marcuse's New Techne

Both Heidegger and Marcuse argue that the normative dimension of techne is eclipsed in modern technology. In this early courses Heidegger explained that the knowledge associated with production does not merely concern means but more fundamentally the rightful outcome of productive activity. That outcome, the ergon or finished work, is present in the means and directs them toward the realization of an eidos or essence. Unlike modern technology, techne is not value neutral knowledge but transcends the opposition of ought and is. This contrast returned after the war in Heidegger's "Question Concerning Technology." Greek techne brings forth pre-existing essences and allows them to manifest themselves in the world whereas modern technology imposes plans on a reality reduced to bare raw materials.

It seems likely that Marcuse's understanding of technology was shaped by these concepts and in fact there are several positive references to this aspect of Heidegger's thought in Marcuse's later work (e.g. Marcuse, 1964, 153-154). There is, however, a subtle difference in emphasis. Under the influence of Hegel, Marcuse explained the concept of essence in terms of the role of potentiality or "real possibility." Essences are the highest realization of what appears imperfectly in the world. Thus essences are in some sense ideals, but not for that matter merely subjective. Essences are objects of striving of the things themselves, historical tendencies. In this reinterpretation of Greek ontology, the concept of truth applies not just to propositions but to things, which can be more or less true to their essential nature.

Marcuse argued that the Greeks misread such tendencies naively in terms of the culturally relative assumptions of their time. The modern discovery of the constructive power of the subject stands in the way of a return to such an uncritical relation to culture. This constructive power is now exercised not only in the spiritual domain of culture but materially, through technology, which transforms the environment according to human plans and purposes. Modern society dismisses the essences of antiquity as obstacles to the free exercise of human powers. Technical means are stripped of any relation to an objective "truth" of the object they create. The new norms under which technology stands are reduced to the formal requirements of domination and, ultimately, of capital as a dynamic force.

This formulation recapitulates in a socially concrete form the basic point of Heidegger's critique of technology, i.e. the radical deworlding accomplished by modernity which shows up in the reification of society to which the individuals are called to submit. The new conformism consists not in obedience to a leader or to customs but more fundamentally in submission to the "facts of life" interpreted one-dimensionally as the only possible organization of a modern society. In so adapting the individuals fall into the objectivistic worship of the given which authentic decision must resist.

Marcuse developed this argument as a historical account of the destiny of reason. This account was shared by other members of the Frankfurt School although only Marcuse proposed a positive alternative. In this tradition the equivalent of Heideggerian techne is what Horkheimer called "objective reason," a reason that incorporates substantive goals (Horkheimer, 1947). The origin of reason in the practical necessities of life is clear in this original objective form. Marcuse could thus argue that reason from the very beginning was rooted in a value judgment, a preference for life over death (Marcuse, 1964: 220). The emergence of modern scientific-technical rationality, Horkheimer's "subjective reason," appears as a reduction of the earlier form of rationality. When substantive goals are removed from the structure of rationality, only means are left: reason becomes instrumental.

This transformation of reason is reflected in the methodology of the sciences and eventually of all the academic disciplines. Reality is analyzed exclusively under those empirical aspects that expose it to calculation and control. The teleological concept of essence is expelled from science; nature is revealed as an object of technology and along with it human beings too are incorporated into a smoothly functioning social machine. This is the basis of the academic world Heidegger hoped to reform with his new beginning. Marcuse rather looked forward to a return of the "objective" dimension of rationality in a future socialist society.

Where Heidegger withdrew from history after his disappointment with Hitler, Marcuse persisted in attempting to rethink the socialist alternative in philosophical terms.[8] To the theme of authenticity as transcendence of objectivism he now added a theory of technological transformation as the material base of socialism. Humane goals must once again be intrinsic to reason, if not in the form of ancient essences in some new form appropriate to the modern age.

These goals cannot be merely subjective but must be disclosed to the subject in the sense that they must have a validating ground that a reason shaped by modernity can recognize and accept. We appear to have returned to Heidegger's problematic of 1933 in search of a better solution than a Führer. Did Marcuse find that solution?

His most explicit attempt to do so was presented in the last chapters of *One-Dimensional Man*. There Marcuse outlined the preconditions of a modern objective reason. He argued that modern science only appears value neutral when artificially separated from its social context. In that larger social context the means it supplies are bound up with the practice and the goals of the dominant social subject. Concretely, value neutrality means the overthrow of all restraints on power. Thus,

> ... it is precisely its neutral character which relates objectivity to a specific historical Subject... Theoretical reason, remaining pure and neutral, entered into the service of practical reason. The merger proved beneficial to both. Today, domination perpetuates and extends itself not only through technology but *as* technology, and the latter provides the great legitimation of the expanding political power, which absorbs all sphere of culture (Marcuse, 1964: 156, 158).

However, Marcuse did not suggest that we abandon modern science and technology. The cognitive advance made possible by the destruction of the old objective reason is undeniable but so is the danger of spiritual and material extermination represented by modern technology unrestrained by any limits.

If subjective reason is not really neutral, neither are rational goals merely subjective. It is possible to restore the unity of ends and means in a modern context. This would be the equivalent of the creation of a modern techne and in fact Marcuse argued that the link between art and craft in antiquity can be restored in a new form. A technology can be devised that pursues idealizing strategies similar to those of art. Misery, injustice, suffering and disorder shall not just be stripped out of the artistic image of the beautiful, but removed practically from existence by appropriate technological solutions to human problems.

Obscure as this abstract formulation appears to be, it corresponds fairly closely with the way we usually think about certain technical professions such as medicine. Marcuse appears to call for a similar professionalization of the whole technological realm.[9] This has implications for technological design since each technical discipline would, like medicine, have an overarching mission. Designs would embody the values implied in that mission and not be subject to the mere will to power of government and business. This, I believe, is how we can understand his demand that values "operate in the project and in the construction of the machinery, and not only in its utilization" (Marcuse, 1964: 232).This would require the reconstruction of the technical base of society.

> This is the notion of the rupture with the continuum of domination, the qualitative difference of socialism as a new form and way of life, not only rational development of the productive forces, but also the redirection of progress toward the ending of the competitive struggle for existence, not only abolition of poverty and toil, but also reconstruction of the social and natural environment as a peaceful, beautiful universe: *total transvaluation of values, transformation of needs and goals.* This implies *still another change in the concept of revolution,* a break with the continuity of the technical apparatus of productivity which, for Marx, would extend (freed from capitalist abuse) to the socialist society. Such *"technological" continuity would constitute a fateful link between capitalism and socialism, because this apparatus has, in its very structure and scope, become an apparatus of control and domination. Cutting this link would mean, not to regress in the technical progress, but to reconstruct the technical apparatus in accordance with the needs of free men...* (Marcuse, 1970: 280).

But is Marcuse out of the woods with these proposals? Not quite. The attempt to reintroduce a notion of privation to which a rational techne would respond with appropriate remedies implies an ontology Marcuse did not develop. Scientific naturalism is not suited for this purpose, nor is it plausible to return to Aristotle. The alternative at which Marcuse hinted was a phenomenology of aesthetic experience in a very broad sense. But although there are indications in his work of how he might have developed such an alternative, he did not work out his aesthetic in sufficient depth and detail to successfully challenge the pessimism of Adorno or Heidegger.

Instead, Marcuse turned to a rather formalistic argument that relied on the existential validity of the new aesthetic sensibility for at least some marginal groups. The basis of this new sensibility, he believed, was an immanent critique of the society, contrasting its ideals and its achievements. As Marcuse pointed out, this contrast grows ever more scandalous as the rising productivity of technology removes the material alibis for poverty, discrimination and war.

This argument then grounded the new techne in a rational judgment able to supply the criteria of a "transcendent project," a progressive development beyond the existing society. The criteria include technical feasibility at the given level of knowledge and technology, and moral desirability in terms of the preservation and enhancement of human freedom and happiness. Furthermore, the transcendent project's rationality would have to be demonstrated through a persuasive analysis and critique of the existing society (Marcuse, 1964: 220).

Technology and Lifeworld

Looking back now from the perspective of the new century, Marcuse's general position remains convincing primarily in this last respect. As analysis and critique *One-Dimensional Man* is unsurpassed despite a generation of efforts to elaborate philosophies of "difference" on the basis of French theory and Adorno. The retreat from the concrete represented by these latter sources is distressingly reminiscent of the false promise of concreteness in Heidegger's work.

What has proven fatal to Marcuse's reputation is his hopeful argument for radical social and technical transformation. Yet this aspect of his work is relevant in a new period of crisis and protest largely focused around technical issues such as environmental pollution, energy politics, and the globalization of industrialization and disease. In this and the concluding parts, therefore, I will consider some starting points for continuing the general line of argument Marcuse developed under the contradictory influences of Heidegger, Marxism and the New Left.

Heidegger and Marcuse argued that the understanding of beings in general, what we would normally call "culture," is rooted in the form of the instrumental relation to reality. That form evolves historically and in its latest incarnation takes on a particularly destructive aspect. The danger is not merely physical but concerns the substitution of technological rationality for every other type of thought. The subject in a "one-dimensional society" neither understands its own essential involvement in its world nor the potentialities with which that world is fraught. Understanding this "second" dimension requires a thought freed from narrow instrumental purposes and capable of addressing lived experience in all its complexity.

These thinkers appear to postulate the existence of a culture – modern technological culture – that evacuates the second dimension. In this technological culture, abstract aspects of social processes are isolated and privileged as the ends of action. The pursuit of ends with means, preferably technically efficient means, replaces an understanding of the structure of meaning in which experienced worlds consist. The focus on the means leads to a forgetfulness of meaning and eventually to the lopping off of whole dimensions of the original experience that appear functionally irrelevant. From within technological culture it seems that all that has been lost in the disenchantment of the world is arbitrary prejudices and myths. According to this view modern scientific-technical rationality supplies all the truth human beings can possibly require. The lifeworld is a poor source of knowledge until its givens have been refined to remove illusory subjective elements. Everything, including human beings, belongs to the technical system. Both Heidegger and Marcuse were tempted at least rhetorically to accept such a reductionist vision as accomplished fact while giving it a dystopian twist: the triumph of Brave New World.

Yet ultimately neither believed the experiential realm could be wholly eliminated. Heidegger claimed that behind the functional appearances of modern technology there lies a mysterious revealing of new meanings which are still hidden to us but which may someday be revealed. Marcuse concluded that the very meaninglessness of modern technology situates it within the project of a ruling class. The destruction of all traditional meaning, which is the condition of capitalist technical and economic advance, is simply the other side of the coin of the reinterpretation of meaning in the degraded form of consumer goods.

In his later work, Marcuse, as we have seen, argued for transforming technology itself. He did not share Heidegger's belief that the relationship to technology could be independent of its design. The particular examples Marcuse cites are the assembly line and advanced weaponry. If these technologies remain at the core of modern life, no change in our relation to them can save us. The movement would thus have to overcome not just the cultural, economic and political orders but the underlying technology of destruction, indifferent to nature, human life and the development of human capacities. But Marcuse could only hint very generally at how this would come about and what the new technology might entail.

Because both thinkers faced a world in which no alternative appeared at the technical level proper, they sought sources of resistance in other domains such as Nazi politics or New Left protest. But this is a departure from the ontologically fundamental role technical practice holds in their own philosophies which they did not adequately explain or justify. These thinkers ended up with such unsatisfactory conclusions because they could find no way to return to the realm of everyday technical experience to discover there the enactment of new meanings that cannot be treated as merely arbitrary, that appeal precisely to a modern ground while pointing beyond the current limitations of modern societies. If we can find a closer connection between politics and technology, a more convincing alternative may appear.

We are in a better position to address this problem than were these predecessors. In Heidegger's and Marcuse's day, it was widely assumed that technical issues should be resolved by experts rather than publicly discussed. Their radical response to these technocratic pretensions was a global critique of technology as such. Both sides in this argument have lost plausibility as a vital politics of technology has emerged around environmental and medical issues, while the rise of the Internet has changed attitudes and opened new avenues for agency in the technical sphere.

Nevertheless, Heidegger's and Marcuse's attempts to restore the cognitive and normative value of the experienced world is still of interest. As in the phenomenological concept of the Lebenswelt, the lived world, so in Marcuse's concept of nature, value and fact are not separate but fused in immediate experience. Our original encounter with nature, both external nature and human nature, is not objectivistic. In everyday practice we always work with "materials" that possess meaning and seek form. Marcuse calls this the "existential" truth of nature, writing, "The emancipation of man involves the recognition of such truth in things, in nature" (Marcuse, 1972: 69).

Elsewhere he carries this phenomenological argument unhesitatingly to the startling conclusion that there are "forces in nature that have been distorted and suppressed – forces which could support and enhance the liberation of man" (Marcuse, 1969: 66). Marcuse was thinking primarily of natural beauty, which he saw as symbol and bearer of peace and happiness, the affirmation of life as a supreme value. Perhaps we can find a less romantic equivalent in those aspects of the natural world that sustain a rich and varied civilization. Some of these are so obvious as to seem trivial – clean air, abundant water, a climate suitable for agriculture and human life – and yet they are being destroyed by uncontrolled development. These benign forces of nature were recognized as such and celebrated by primitive peoples. Respect for such forces is still required from us moderns. It should take the form of less destructive strategies of development.

It would be easy to dismiss these speculations as naïve attempts at re-enchantment of what science has thoroughly disenchanted. But phenomenology is not naively metaphysical. Data of prereflective experience everyone can verify for themselves support the idea of an "existential truth" of nature. The dismissal of the experiential realm as "merely subjective" is ethnocentric as the discussion of Heidegger in the first part of this paper attempted to show. While there are no obstacles in principle to the indefinite extension of research into nature, the claim that nature as science understands it is the one and only reality has no scientific basis. Experience is not reducible to its natural conditions as a reductionist naturalism would have us believe. Narrow scientism borrows the prestige of real science for a dubious philosophy.

Worlds of experience are contingent in their details but have an essential structure that is presupposed by objective understanding of nature. Heidegger merely alludes to this point which he seems to think is obvious, but it is further developed by Karl-Otto Apel as a "transcendental-pragmatic" grounding of science in practice. According to Apel, science presupposes human action through which scientific data are gathered. Experiments, which create closed domains within which laws can be observed to operate, themselves depend on action. But action is only understandable as such, that is, as meaningful, from a phenomenological or hermeneutic standpoint distinct from that of natural science. If action is reduced to its natural conditions, for example, certain muscular reflexes, it is de-worlded and no longer makes sense. The totalization of science in a naturalistic reductionism would eliminate action and so render the possibility of scientific understanding itself unintelligible. In this sense action is a quasi-transcendental precondition of (scientific) knowledge. Apel thus argues for a "complementarity" of hermeneutic understanding and scientific explanation (Apel, 1984: 63-64).

But Apel's argument is incomplete. His thesis according to which meaningful action is a precondition of scientific knowledge depends on the still more fundamental thesis that the world as the network of meaningful objects is the precondition of action. For action to make sense it must address objects that themselves possess significance. The essential structures of action must correlate with essential structures of objects as they are found in lived experience. The lifeworld extends into the practical realm as a whole and does not concern action alone as appears to be the case in Apel's formulation. But this means that it is not only action which escapes reduction, but objects as well.

This observation has implications for technology which, like scientific experiment, exists on both sides of the line separating the lifeworld from the order of natural causality. Technologies are at one and the same time meaningful within the lifeworld and functional as causal mechanisms. Their two-sidedness is essential to their very being, and is not an external combination of subjective feelings and objective things. Meaning is thus the precondition not just of the scientific rationality but also of technology's very existence within a lived world.[10]

A phenomenological concept of meaning is found in several Heideggerian analyses of ancient Greek poiesis and more abstractly formulated in *Being and Time.* For our purposes, the most significant proposals concern the role of essence which Heidegger develops in some detail in his course on Aristotle's *Metaphysics,* and which he takes up again in condensed form in "The Question Concerning Technology."

Essences consist in the form and purpose of the materials. But form and purpose are precisely what has been reduced to arbitrary plans in modern times. Yet there is a dimension of essence that retains a deeper validity, that is not subject to arbitrary manipulation. Recall that essences are by nature limitations on the formless materials from which the produced thing is made. As Heidegger writes, "The end which finishes, however, is in its essence, boundary, peras. To produce something is in itself to forge something into its boundaries... Every work is in its essence 'exclusive' (a fact for which we barbarians for a long time now lack the facility)" (Heidegger, 1995: 118). On this Greek model, no culture can exist without some notion of meaning, that is, as Heidegger describes it here, some limit on the infinite possibilities of action and objects.

Heidegger's notion of essential limits merits further exploration in a modern context. It is here that we encounter the peculiar ingression of objectivity into experience that corresponds to Apel's account of the foundational role of experience in science. Limits emerge in the lifeworld as objective knowledge feeds back into experience, guiding it toward demands for less destructive technological designs. Thus the complementarity of objectivity and experience Apel identifies is not just cognitive but has political implications as well. This has to do with the structure of technical action as it has developed in modern times.

Structures of Action

Technical action involves a hidden oscillation between reason and experience that can be made explicit in a transcendental-pragmatic account paralleling in the practical domain Apel's account of science. This oscillation can be clarified on systems theoretic terms by distinguishing a finite actor from a hypothetical infinite actor capable of a "do from nowhere."[11] The latter can act on its object without reciprocity. God creates the world without suffering any recoil, side effects, or blowback. This is the ultimate practical hierarchy establishing a one way relation between actor and object. Modern thought takes this imaginary relation as the model of rationality and objectivity, the point at which practice transcends itself in pure theory. But in reality we are not gods. Human beings can only act on a system to which they themselves belong. This is the practical significance of embodiment and implies participation in a meaningful world. Apel notes the implications of our finitude for knowledge, which depends on action for its acquisition. In practice, finitude shows up as the reciprocity of action and reaction. In this domain every one of our interventions returns to us in some form as feedback from our objects. This is obvious in everyday communication where anger usually evokes anger, kindness kindness, and so on.

The technical subject does not escape from the logic of finitude, but the reciprocity of finite action is dissipated or deferred in such a way as to create the space of a necessary illusion of transcendence. Technical action represents a partial escape from the human condition. We call an action "technical" when the actor's impact on the object is out of all proportion to the return feedback affecting the actor. We hurtle two tons of metal down the freeway while sitting in comfort listening to Mozart or the latest pop music. This typical instance of technical action is purposely framed here to dramatize the independence of actor from object. In the larger scheme of things, the driver on the freeway may be at peace in his car but the city he inhabits with millions of other drivers is his life environment and it is shaped by the automobile into a type of place that has major impacts on him.

Heidegger understands the illusion of technique as the structure of modern experience. While objects enter experience only in so far as they are useful in the technological system, the subject appears as pure disincarnated rationality, methodically controlling and planning as though external to its own world. For Heidegger, release from this form of experience may come from a new mode of revealing but he has no idea how revealings come and go. Like Marcuse, I relate the technological revealing not to the history of being, but to the consequences of persisting divisions between classes and between rulers and ruled in technically mediated institutions of all types.

As I reformulate this social version of the technical revealing, it has political consequences. Political protests arise as feedback from disastrous technical projects and designs reaches those excluded from the original networks of control. These protests are often based on scientific knowledge of the devastation caused by technology designed in indifference to human needs. This is the point at which objective facts enter experience as motives for distrust and fear of technology and technical authority. The subjects become aware of the contingency of the technically structured world on choices and decisions that do not proceed from a supposedly pure rationality. The lifeworld reacts back on technology through the objective contents of knowledge of its side effects.

There have been many attempts to articulate the implications of this new situation. My approach is closest to that of Ulrich Beck. Like him I argue that we are entering a new phase of technological development in which the externalities associated with the prevailing technologies threaten the survival of the industrial system (Beck, 1992). This threat has begun to force redesign of many technologies and changes in the disciplines and training underlying the technical professions. Beck explains the transition from a capitalism based on distinct spheres with little interaction, to a "reflexive modernity" in which interaction between spheres becomes the norm. Multiple approaches and cross disciplinary conceptions increasingly shape the design process in response. He develops the social consequences of the resultant changes while I have focused primarily on the technological dimension of the new phase.

In this phase, what Gilbert Simondon calls "concretizing" innovations emerge designed to accommodate a wider range of social influences and contextual factors.[12] As design is pulled in different directions by actors attempting to impose their differing functional requirements on devices, the winning design strategies are often those that reconcile multiple functions in simple and elegant structures capable of serving them all. Examples abound: hybrid engines in automobiles, refrigerants and propellants that do not damage the ozone layer, substitutes for lead in consumer products, and so on. In the process of developing these technologies environmental, medical and other concerns are brought to bear on design by new actors excluded from the original technological regime. Of course, no small refinements such as these can resolve the environmental crisis, but the fact that they are possible at all removes the threat of technological regression as a major alibi for doing nothing.

The emergence of a radically new technical politics requires us to rethink the basic concept of rationality that has supplied the existing industrial society with its highest philosophical sanction. Heidegger and Marcuse help us to understand the limitations of the prevailing concept. They remind us that the hypostatization of a reason fragmented into specializations and differentiated from a broader cultural and normative context is not inevitable but belongs to a specific historical era, an era that may well be approaching its end. A new understanding of rationality is possible based not on a return to a teleological worldview in which we can no longer believe but on recognition of the complexity of experiences that have been cast in artificially narrow instrumental schemas. Concrete experience is thus the touchstone of this ontology because it is only there that the world reveals itself in its multifarious and unpredictable connections and potentialities.

From this new standpoint specialization and differentiation will not disappear, but they will be treated as methodologically useful rather than as ontologically fundamental. The resultant breaching of the boundaries between disciplines and between the technical realm and the lifeworld responds to the crisis of industrial society. We may learn to bound the cosmos in modern forms by attending to the limits that emerge from the unintended interactions of domains touched by powerful modern technologies.

This is the form in which the lived world we have discovered in the thought of Heidegger and Marcuse becomes active in the structure of a rationality that still has for its mission the explanation of objective nature. The discovery of a limit reveals the significance of that which is threatened beyond it. This dialectic of limitation is most obvious in the case of threats to human health or species survival. On the one side, the experienced world gains a ground in respect for an object, in this case the human body or a threatened species. On the other side, a concrete technical response is solicited employing the means at hand in new combinations or inventing new ones. From this standpoint no return to a qualitative science is possible or necessary. Modern science objectifies and reifies by its very nature but it could operate within limits standing in for the lost essences of antiquity and like them referring us to an irreducible truth of experience. As we encounter this truth we are reminded of the necessity of restraint.

This must be a productive restraint leading to a process of transformation, not a passive refusal of a reified system. The forward looking Janus face is fundamental and grants hope not by rejecting scientific-technical achievements but by revealing their essential nature as processes in which human action can intervene.[13] Innovative responses to the new limits can serve in the reconstruction of both technical disciplines and technology. To be sure, the process character and full complexity of reality cannot be reflected immediately in the scientific-technical disciplines, but the disciplines can be deployed in fluid combinations that reflect the complexity of reality as it enters experience through humanly provoked disasters of all sorts and through the consciousness of new threats of which we ourselves are the ultimate source.

The goal is not merely to survive but to reconstruct modern technology around a new model of wealth that is environmentally compatible and that draws on human capacities suppressed or ignored in the present dispensation. Marcuse interpreted this in terms of the surrealist "hazard objectif," the rather fantastic notion of an aesthetically formed world in which "human faculties and desires ... appear as part of the objective determinism of nature – coincidence of causality through nature and causality through freedom" (Marcuse, 1969: 31).

Conclusion

In conclusion I would like to summarize briefly the core of the argument the strands of which I have been following throughout this paper. The concept of essence which prevailed until the scientific revolution gave rational form to the teleological structure of everyday experience. In modern times, the differentiation of scientific-technical rationality from everyday experience split the two formerly interwoven domains into fragments of an unattainable whole. Under this new dispensation, meaning and human ends appear subjective, nature and technical means objective, and no mediation reconciles them. An earlier form of rationality based on a teleological interpretation of experience is irretrievably lost except as a reminder of that impossible reconciliation.

Today we confront a world of artifacts so elaborate and complex that it overshadows our lives in every domain. But this world is not shaped by essences. Its structures correspond to the various fragmented disciplines and organizations that make up modern societies. Until recently it was possible to imagine that the fragmented logic of modernity was without negative consequences. No longer. The environmental crisis that results from the interference between the fragmented domains reveals the complexity of the real world, which does not correspond to the boundaries between the historically evolved disciplines and organizations.

The problem reduced to its simplest terms is the collapse of any notion of rational ends once essences no longer guide practice toward sanctioned results. But this formulation masks the deeper question of the nature of these essences in which we can no longer believe. In premodern societies the concept of essence derives from the making of artifacts according to culturally accepted rules. Essences thus join experience as it is lived in a particular society with technically rational practices that are articulated in theoretical knowledge in modern times. The artifacts themselves face in both directions, on the one hand participating in the normatively informed world of everyday experience, on the other implementing ever more sophisticated rational understanding of nature.

We cannot recover the normativity of technique by a simple act of invention. Norms can only emerge from the shared experience of a community, a world. Worlds in this more or less Heideggerian sense must be understood as realms of practice rather than as a passively observed nature to which "values" are ascribed. Worlds are built out of myriad connections uncovered in the course of everyday experience as Heidegger explains in the suggestive first part of *Being and Time*. These form a horizon within which actions and objects take on meaning. Meanings are not things we have at our disposal, but frameworks, perspectives we inhabit and which contribute to making us what and who we are. Meanings are enacted in our perceptions and practices. They are not chosen but rather they "claim us" from "behind our backs" (Simpson, 1995). What might be the source of such meanings today?

Marcuse argued that reason itself might play this role. Reason has always presupposed a value judgment, the preference for life over death. In ignoring this value judgement, modern societies become unreasonable in their very rationality. Unfortunately, this formulation evokes a rather limited utilitarian framework. I would argue that the elimination of any value judgment from the structure of modern technological rationality, the neutralization of reason, leads to the collapse of the exclusiveness that is a condition for meaningful action. The systematically negative relation of modern technological rationality to meaning is a violation of the requirements of action which, as we have seen, necessarily involves meaning. Technological rationality is thus deficient with respect to the historically evolved concept of reason not only in its indifference to life but, underlying that indifference, in its very structure. Crudely put, when meanings become marketing devices, anything goes and rationality itself is threatened.

What then is the place of meaning in a modern world that has given up on teleology? For the Greeks, telos is the other side of peras. Meaning arises from selection, limitation. What is excluded is the erroneous move that deviates from the essential eidos of the produced thing. Connectedness was acknowledged implicitly in the limitations built into the essences of things. But exclusion in this Greek sense is not just negative; it is the other side of the positive act of production.

For us moderns, who have lost essential discrimination of this sort, another kind of exclusion is nevertheless possible. This new "peras" must make sense in modern scientific terms but cannot be derived from science alone. We hear about such limits now constantly in popular discourse which emphasizes the importance of respect for the natural balance and human health. These are the norms that should determine modern technological design. The hypothesis hazarded by this paper is that the new limits can take the place formerly occupied by essence as a mediation between experience and rationality. The result would be the restoration of a value-laden conception of rationality, a renewed techne, compatible with modern science and reflecting the exigencies of a coherent world of experience.

Our growing sense of the danger of the reified institutions and ever more powerful technologies bequeathed us by several centuries of capitalist progress confronts us with choices in the re-making of the technical world. Even if they have no scientific status, normative concepts such as human health and the balance of nature do not contradict the cognitive advances of modern science but on the contrary require scientific knowledge to evaluate conflicting claims.

At the dawn of the modern era, thinkers such as Descartes and Bacon expected that the new science and technology would be framed by a wisdom restraining human ambitions. Like technology, wisdom too is located between reason and experience. These two modes of thought require each other. This was the original vision of the philosophers who overthrew ancient teleology. But they were unable to find a substitute for essence capable of serving in its place. Perhaps now, at a decisive turning point along the road they opened, we will be able to realize their vision.

References

Angus, Ian (2000). *Primal Scenes of Communication*. Albany, State Univ. of New York Press.
Apel, Karl-Otto (1984). *Understanding and Explanation: A Transcendental-Pragmatic Approach.* Cambridge, Mass.: MIT Press.
Beck, Ulrich (1992). *Risk Society*. London: Sage.
Feenberg, Andrew (1999). *Questioning Technology*. New York: Routledge.
Feenberg, Andrew (2005). *Heidegger and Marcuse: The Catastrophe and Redemption of History.* New York: Routledge.
Foltz, Bruce (1995). *Inhabiting the Earth*. Atlantic Highlands: Humanities Press.
Heidegger, Martin (1962). *Being and Time*, trans. J. Macquarrie & E. Robinson. New York: Harper and Row.
– (1993a). "The Self-Assertion of the German University", in R. Wolin, ed. *The Heidegger Controversy: A Critical Reader*. Cambridge, Mass.: MIT Press.

– (1993b). "Overcoming Metaphysics," trans. J. Stambaugh, in R. Wolin, ed. *The Heidegger Controversy: A Critical Reader*. Cambridge, Mass.: MIT Press.
– (1994). *Basic Questions of Philosophy*, trans. R. Rojcewicz and A. Schuwer. Bloomington and Indianapolis: Indiana University Press.
– (1995). *Aristotle's Metaphysics Θ 1-3: On the Essence and Actuality of Force*, trans. W. Brogan and P. Warnek. Bloomington and Indianapolis: Indiana University Press.
Horkheimer, Max (1947). *Eclipse of Reason*. New York: Seabury Press.
Latour, Bruno (1987). *Science in Action: How to Follow Scientists and Engineers through Society*. Cambridge, Mass.: Harvard.
Lukács, George (1971). *History and Class Consciousness*, trans. R. Livingstone. Cambridge, Mass.: MIT Press.
Marcuse, Herbert (1964). *One-Dimensional Man*. Boston: Beacon Press.
– (1969). *An Essay on Liberation*. Boston: Beacon.
– (1970). "Re-Examination of the Concept of Revolution," in A. Lothstein, ed. *All We Are Saying*. New York: Capricorn Books.
– (1972). *Counter-Revolution and Revolt*. Boston: Beacon.
Nietzsche, Friedrich (1956). *The Birth of Tragedy and the Genealogy of Morals* trans. F. Gollfing. New York: Anchor.
Olafson, Frederick (2007). "Heidegger's Politics: An Interview with Herbert Marcuse," in A. Feenberg and W. Leiss, eds. *The Essential Marcuse*. Boston: Beacon Press.
Pinch, Trevor and Bijker, Wiebe. (1989). "The Social Construction of Facts and Artefacts: or How the Sociology of Science and the Sociology of Technology Might Benefit Each Other," in W. Bijker, T. Hughes, and T. Pinch, eds., *The Social Construction of Technological Systems*. Cambridge, Mass.: MIT Press.
Schürmann, Reiner (1990). *Heidegger on Being and Acting: From Principles to Anarchy*. Bloomington and Indianapolis: Indiana University Press.
Simondon, Gilbert (1958). *Du Mode d'Existence des Objets Techniques*. Paris: Aubier.
Simpson, Lorenzo (1995). *Technology, Time, and the Conversations of Modernity*. New York: Routledge.
Todorov, Tzvetan (2007). "Avant-gardes & totalitarianism," trans. A. Goldhammer, *Daedalus*, Winter 2007.
Whitehead, Alfred North (2004). *The Concept of Nature*. Amherst, New York: Prometheus Books.
Zimmerman, Michael (1990). *Heidegger's Confrontation with Modernity: Technology, Politics, Art*. Bloomington: Indiana Univ. Press.

Notes

1. See also my account of the relation between the thought of Heidegger and Marcuse in Feenberg (2005).
2. This notion has its parallel in the derivation of presence-at-hand from readiness-to-hand in *Being and Time*.
3. For an interesting discussion of such notions, see Todorov (2007).
4. As practical enactment, meaning has a "material" dimension that might be explored in a phenomenology of technical practice and technology. This has implications for the discursive turn in contemporary philosophy. So long as reality is understood as structured by or like a language, it is difficult to account for the passive aspect of knowing. The failure to take into

account the resistance of the object and the facticity of the subject leads discourse theory to an implausible relativism. But if meanings are understood as enacted in a practice, they cannot be merely subjective but must entertain a relation to a materiality of some sort (Angus, 2000: 13). Developing this approach would make sense of the moment of receptivity in such Heideggerian notions as disclosure.

5. A similar contradiction haunts "post-modernity," an era which can only open under the horizon of a modern temporality it professes to reject.
6. The difference between reification and dereification is nicely illustrated by Bruno Latour's notion of the Janus face of science: science in the making and science made (Latour, 1987: 4). These two "faces," the glance into the future and the backward glance toward the past, correspond to an understanding of the social world as a process in which human action plays a role and the reified society that results from that process, standing before the spectator as a fixed and finished objectivity.
7. Walter Benjamin aimed at a similar goal through an appropriation of religious notions rather than philosophical ones, but the result was a comparable recovery of the moral intensity of the revolutionary mission in contrast with the rationalistic scientism of the prevailing social democratic ideology.
8. Heidegger writes, for example, in *Overcoming Metaphysics* that "No mere action will change the world," and in his last interview he resists the suggestion that politics holds out hope and endorses "thinking," which he claims is "not inactivity but is itself the action which stands in dialogue with the world mission" (Heidegger, 1993b: 89; Heidegger, 1993a: 110). No doubt sympathetic readers of Heidegger will disagree with my characterization of such statements as "withdrawal." Yet I find no evidence in any of Heidegger's texts that he seriously envisaged a reform program. The conclusion to Michael Zimmerman's book on Heidegger reviews many attempts to understand the later Heidegger's view of technology and concludes persuasively that we must criticize his "presupposition about the extent to which human beings are incapable of resisting and developing alternatives to that [technological] disclosure" (Zimmerman, 1990: 268).
9. It might be objected that professional organizations have their own narrow interests and are easily manipulated by political or economic power. Obviously what is interesting about this model is not its current institutional form but its cognitive structure. Professionalization by itself has no power to solve the problems of society. Its significance depends on the context in which it functions.
10. This is the import of the instrumentalization theory explained in more detail in Feenberg (1999: chap. 7).
11. The implied reference is to the concept of a godlike "view from nowhere." If it were not too cute, one might rephrase the point here as a "do from knowhere," i.e. action understood as just as indifferent to its objects as detached knowing.
12. See Simondon (1958: chap. 1) and Feenberg (1991: 191ff). Simondon illustrates his concept of concretization with examples of politically neutral innovations such as the air-cooled engine, which combines cooling with containment through the design of the engine case, two functions in one structure. I have modified his approach to take into account what we have learned from social studies of technology about the social forces behind technical functions. For example, Pinch and Bijker show how the inflatable tire enabled an inherently more stable but slower bicycle design to overcome its disadvantage in bicycle racing while retaining the stability that made it attractive for transportation (Pinch and Bijker, 1989: 44-46). Two different social groups, young men interested in speed and ordinary riders engaged in everyday usages, were reconciled in this innovation.

13. It is discouraging to note that such reflections are often criticized as "optimistic." Fundamental historical transformations are not subject to calculations of probability. Dogmatic pessimism is as thoughtless as its contrary, uncritical optimism. Neither attitude is helpful in understanding the contradictory process of technological change we are witnessing. For that, analytic tools rather than attitudes are required. What the analysis shows is a convergence of increasing public demands for better technology and a new conception of technology as social and responsive to a wide range of constraints. Although by no means powerful enough to prevail at this time, these trends cannot be ignored.

REMARKS ON WITTGENSTEIN'S PHILOSOPHY: PRIVATE LANGUAGE AND MEANING

Kaj Børge Hansen

University of Uppsala

ABSTRACT. This essay is a critical analysis of some themes in Wittgenstein's later philosophy. It is not primarily Wittgenstein-exegesis. Much more modestly, my purpose is to express my own thoughts about some questions which Wittgenstein has treated in his writings. It is the first in a series of two articles. The second article, "Remarks on Wittgenstein's Philosophy: Philosophical Method and Contradictions", will occur in next year's issue of the present Yearbook.

Section 1, "The Private Language Argument". An independent argument is given for Wittgenstein's thesis that there is no private language. I show that psychological terms in ordinary language, in contrast to an implication of Wittgenstein's own private language argument, in their meanings do contain references to inner states, processes, or events.

Section 2, "Meaning". Wittgenstein's definition of meaning as use in the language is criticised. Meaning is instead identified with something in the content of a conscious mind. Applications are given to some suggestions in philosophy of language by Chomsky, Grice, Harman and Fodor, and Kripke.

For orientation, I also include here the abstract for the second article, "Remarks on Wittgenstein's Philosophy: Philosophical Method and Contradictions".

Section 1, "Philosophical Method". Wittgenstein's conception of philosophy as language therapy is criticised. Instead philosophy is construed as foundational research. Wittgenstein's statement that mathematical logic cannot contribute to progress in philosophy is repudiated. Several examples of ideas and results in mathematical logic which have led to the solution of philosophical problems are given.

Section 2, "Contradictions: The Wittgenstein-Turing Debate". In lectures on the foundations of mathematics given in 1939, Wittgenstein claimed that contradictions in mathematical theories are harmless. A debate ensued on this question between him and Alan Turing. In support of Turing's standpoint, I use the theorem on Taylor series, Church's Theorem, and Gentzen's Cut-Elimination Theorem to show that Wittgenstein's standpoint is untenable.

1. The Private Language Argument

1.1 **Anthropology.** I assume that a human being at any time is a well-defined system. He consists of a body and has a central nervous system, including a brain. I assume that a human being has the capacity of self-awareness (or self-consciousness). The body and the central nervous system can be studied from the outside, for instance by the methods of physiology, psychology, neurology, and molecular biology. The self-awareness implies that the individual, at least to some extent, is aware of himself as a system of limited spatial extension, of his body and its parts and of their function. I also assume that self-awareness implies a *direct* consciousness in the individual of some of the states, processes, and events in his own central nervous system. Thus the body and the central nervous system, and in particular the brain, can also be studied from the inside, via introspection. As a consequence we can know a lot about our own brain independently of whether we know that we have a brain and which biological properties it has. Self-awareness even implies an understanding of the fact that other individuals of the same species, Homo Sapiens, have similar bodies and brains as one self and are self-aware and self-conscious.

1.2 REMARK. Some of Wittgenstein's statements in his later philosophy have been interpreted to mean that he did not agree with the claim that self-awareness implies a *direct* consciousness in the individual of states, processes, and events in his own central nervous system. Instead he might have had a behaviourist view to the effect that we only have indirect knowledge of what is going on in our brains and central nervous systems via observation of our own behaviour and tendency to behaviour. Whatever may have been Wittgenstein's view, I myself believe in our direct awareness of our central nervous systems (and will use it freely in the present essay) for the following reasons.

(1) Sometimes we dream during sleep and remember the dream when we wake up. We remember the dream as a vivid visual observation of a scene. A similar vivid fantasy could not be constructed by the brain from observations of our own behaviour immediately after waking up. This shows that we have been directly aware of the inner activity going on during the dreaming. Thus a direct awareness of an inner process is, indeed, possible and can be assumed to be present in the case of other mental states and processes as well.

(2) Self-awareness has been shown to be present in the following species apart from Homo Sapiens: the primates (chimpanzees, bonobos, orangutangs, and gorillas), dolphins, and elephants. Self-awareness, including awareness of states etc. in ones own body and brain, is clearly a very useful faculty in the struggle for life. If such an awareness is direct, it can be attained in a fragment of a second. If the awareness were indirect, it should be much slower and much less useful in critical situations than it actually is.

1.3 DEFINITION. In *Philosophische Untersuchungen*, Wittgenstein investigates the idea of a private language in §§243-309, and with a definition of the concept in §269. A *private language* is a language which, even in principle, is impossible to understand by anybody except a single user U of the language.

1.4 **First Thesis.** Wittgenstein asks whether there is any private language. His first claim is:

(4-1)   *There is not and cannot be any private language.*

I agree with this thesis and now give my own argument for it.

1.5 **The Church-Turing Thesis.** (1) An arithmetical function is computable iff it is recursive.

(2) Every algorithm, whether numerical or non-numerical, can be represented by a recursive function.

I assume the Church-Turing thesis and use it freely in the sequel.

1.6 ANALYSIS. The following seems to be a reasonable characterisation of some essential features of all languages.

A language $L = (E, F)$ consists of a set E containing all the expressions of the language (for instance, words, phrases, and sentences) and a semantic function F which to every expression in E assigns a meaning. If some of the expressions are homonyms, F must be multiple-valued. A user U must be able to recognise the expressions in E and distinguish them from other objects not belonging to E. This implies that the characteristic function K_E of E must be recursive. To understand the language L, U must have and master a complete definition of the semantic function F. This implies that F must be determined by a finite rule which can be and is stored in U's memory and which can be followed by U in the calculation of F. Therefore, according to the Church-Turing thesis, F must be a recursive function. (It can be argued that K_E and F must be primitive recursive functions; but we do not need this fact in the present essay.)

1.7 ARGUMENT. I give my own argument for the thesis 1.4 on the non-existence of a private language. Suppose that the user U masters the language L = (E, F). I now show that it is possible, at least in principle, for another individual R to understand L. As part of the definition of the problem assigned to R, he is given the syntactic part of the language, that is, he is informed about the characteristic function K_E. His task is to try to figure out a definition of the semantic function F. We note that since U masters the semantic function F, U has a complete definition of F as a recursive function in his memory. R can study U's brain from the outside and he can, in principle, obtain sufficiently much information about the content of U's memory so that he has a complete definition of F. The memory of a computer can be scanned from the outside and the information in the memory examined. We are not forced to use the computer's own scanning function. I see no reason why it should not similarly in principle be possible to scan the memory of a human being from the outside and examine his or her knowledge. The fact that it is knowledge about meaning makes no difference. What is so special about knowledge of meaning? Equipped with F, also R will be able to understand L which is then not private. (Using a similar way of reasoning, one can refute Wittgenstein's dictum that if a lion could speak, we should not be able to understand the lion.)

1.8 REMARK. Let L be a language fragment used by U. The most common method used for another person V to reach an understanding of L is via an *interpretation I*. U can to some extent via the self-awareness look into his own central nervous system, including how the expressions of L are associated with meaning. V has no such privileged access. For him, U's mind is a black box.

V's interpretation consists in formulating a theory about the black box. It is a theory about how expressions in L are connected with meaning. The formulation of theories about black boxes is a well-known type of problems in the sciences. Thus for instance the atomic nucleus can be considered a black box and nuclear physics is the theory about the inner structure of this black box. Characteristic of black box theories is that they cannot be verified; but they can in principle be falsified, and this suffices to make the enterprise meaningful and scientific. This is also how theologians, philologists, and historians of philosophy work: formulate hypotheses of interpretation and try to falsify them. Wittgenstein demands (§258 in *Philosophische Untersuchungen*) that an interpretation must involve a criterion by which the correctness of the association of symbol with meaning can be shown to be correct. I suppose that the criterion must be possible to *apply* to decide whether the association is correct, that is, whether the expressions of L are used correctly. Then the criterion is an algorithm. This implies that an interpretation must be verifiable; but this is too strong a demand on a black box theory, both in physics and in semantics. Falsifiability suffices.

1.9 REMARK. Wittgenstein's own argumentation for Thesis 1.4 is very different. There is some uncertainty about what he meant by the private language argument. In this section, I will proceed by taking his statements and examples for what I consider to be their face value. In Section 2, I will briefly consider another, weaker interpretation. When Wittgenstein draws conclusions from the private language argument, he seemingly uses the stronger interpretation considered in the present section. Therefore it will be our main alternative. In the argument, he takes what he apparently considers to be a proposal for a private language: the fragment of language concerned with pain and other sensations. He then tries to show that such expressions do not in their meanings contain components which refer to something inner and private (inner and private in the mental sense). Thereby he assumes that if an expression belonging to psychological language, for instance an expression concerned with a sensation, has a reference to something inner and private, it cannot be understood by anybody else than the user U and therefore is a private language. This assumption is not trivial; and it will turn out actually to be false. It turns out that psychological terms do refer to inner states, processes, and events in the mind, and they do it in the same way that physical terms refer to states, processes, and events in the external, physical world.

1.10 **Second Thesis.** Thus Wittgenstein has a second thesis:

(10-1)   *Expressions belonging to philosophical psychology, for instance expressions concerned with sensations, do not in their meanings contain a reference to inner and private states, processes, or events.*

1.11 QUOTATION. "How are words *related* to sensations? [...] For instance the word 'pain'. The following is a possibility: Words are connected with the original, natural expression of the sensation and replace it. A child has hurt himself, he cries; then the grown-ups talk to him and teach him exclamations and later sentences. They teach the child a new pain behaviour. [...] the verbal expression of pain replaces the crying and does not describe it." (*PhU*, §244)

(* The quotations in sections 1 and 2 from *Philosophische Untersuchungen* are my own translations into English.*)

1.12 REMARK. Thus Wittgenstein claims that expressions like "I have pain", "I have a headache", and "It hurts in my left knee when I walk" really are only a kind of pain behaviour on a par with crying or groaning. It does happen incidentally that such expressions are used the way Wittgenstein claims. Thus it has happened that I, as a kind of groaning, have said "It hurts, oh, it hurts so much" at occasions when I have hurt myself against something. But it is hard to believe that his claim is generally true. For example:

(1) The child already has a natural register of pain behaviour consisting in crying and groaning. What is the idea of expanding the register?

(2) Crying and groaning are generally quite inarticulate. Many uses of expressions for pain and other sensations are in contrast very detailed and specific. Examples occur when we see a doctor and try to give as precise a description of our symptoms as possible. There a patient might talk to the physician as follows: "I have a strong headache. It is like a heavy pressure over the forehead. It is particularly intense in the morning. It decreases somewhat during the day and is slightly better in the evening. Still the pain makes it difficult for me to fall asleep in the evening, and I usually wake up two or three times during the night because of the pain. It is getting a little worse every day. The headache started c. six weeks ago; and during the last 2-3 weeks, it has been a real ordeal I dare say." The language used is descriptive rather than expressive. The patient's attitude is one of observation and recollection. The procedure is much

more similar to the description of something in space and time than it is to groaning. It is as if he is describing an inner state.

For this reason I find the following to be a more reasonable picture.

(12-1) *Expressions in the language used for pain, feelings, sensations, perceptions, fantasies, dreams, thoughts, ideas etc. refer to inner states, processes, or events, and this reference is an essential component in the meaning of the expressions.*

Thus I adhere to this unsophisticated common sense view as opposed to Wittgenstein's sophisticated philosophical view. I now review and analyse some of Wittgenstein's arguments against Thesis (12-1) and also some arguments against the same thesis and for Thesis (10-1) advanced by other philosophers. During the process, my own reasons for believing in Thesis (12-1) will become clear.

1.13 QUOTATION. "To what extent are my sensations *private?* – Well, only I can know whether I really have pain; another person can only presume it. – This is in one way false and in another way nonsense. When we use the word 'know' as it is normally used (and in what other way should we else use it!), then other people very often know when I have pain." (§246)

1.14 REMARK. My sensations are private to the extent in which I have access to them and other people do not. Via the self-awareness, I often know immediately about my own pain while other people do not. In principle, it is possible for other people by studying my body and central nervous system from the outside to know everything about my pain. But under the circumstances which normally characterise human social life, most of the methods and equipment needed for such investigations are not available. In particular, they are not present in the circumstances under which we acquire a language. Every normally developed person has via the self-awareness a privileged access to immediate knowledge about states and processes in his own central nervous system. It cannot apriori be excluded that this privileged access plays a role in the way we learn a language and the meaning we assign to linguistic symbols.

1.15 QUOTATION. "Of myself, it is not at all possible that I say (except possibly as a joke) that I *know* that I have pain. What is that supposed to mean – except possibly that I *have* pain." (§246)

1.16 REMARK. The linguistic usage of the word "pain" is not as unambiguous as Wittgenstein claims. In one usage, I can have pain without knowing it. In another usage, having pain implies knowing that one has pain so that they are one and the same thing.

(1) "I know that I have pain" can mean that I am conscious of my pain. Via the self-awareness, it is possible to be directly conscious of a pain. But it is also possible at times not to know of a pain though it is there, for instance because my attention at that moment is totally occupied with something else or because the self-awareness is absent. Thus a person can have pain when he is sleeping and not know about it because his self-awareness during sleep is turned off. The pain can be inferred from his behaviour during the sleep by people observing him, for instance from his groaning while sleeping. In this sense of "pain", pain is a state Π in the brain of which one may be or not be aware.

(2) There are also people who are only willing to ascribe pain to a person who is aware of the pain. For them, a person can have no pain during the sleep no matter how much he groans and shows other pain behaviour. In this sense of "pain", pain is the kind of state Σ in the brain which consists in a direct awareness of a state of type Π.

I am interested in showing that words like "pain" can – and do – refer to inner states. Wittgenstein's argument in Quotation 1.15, if it is meant as an argument, does not help to exclude this possibility. Because in the first sense of "pain", the word refers to an inner state of type Π. In its second sense, "pain" refers to an inner state of type Σ.

1.17 QUOTATION. "Let us imagine the following case. I want to keep a journal of how a certain sensation recurs. For this purpose I associate it with the symbol "S" and write this symbol in a calendar every day when I have the sensation. – I first want to call attention to the fact that no definition of the symbol can be formulated. – But I can still give it to myself as a kind of ostensive definition! – How? Can I point to the sensation?" (§258)

1.18 REMARK. It is a misunderstanding to believe that pointing is part of an ostensive definition. When we, in order to define a phenomenon to a person P by an ostensive definition, point to the pertinent instance of the phenomenon, the sole function of the pointing is to draw P's attention to the instance. If we are certain that P at the moment already gives sufficient attention to the phenomenon, we can give the ostensive definition without pointing first. Similarly in Wittgenstein's example, if my attention is already focused on the sensation, or the memory of the sensation – and whether this is the case or not, I can decide via the self-awareness – then an ostensive definition can be given without any previous pointing.

The way we teach children words for different kinds of pain follows this pattern. We wait until the child has become a victim of some kind of pain and we are certain that the pain fills his or her attention. Then we comfort the child by, among other things, speaking to him or her and using words for the relevant kind of pain. I was myself a witness to the following episode. One evening, I visited a couple who had a little son, Johannes, two years old. A candle was lighted on the table. Johannes got curious about the fire and climbed up on the table via a chair. To examine the light, he tried to stick his right index finger into the flame and got burned. He started immediately to cry and the tears flowed. The parents were quickly in place and comforted him and spoke to him: "Have you hurt yourself, Johannes? Oh, you burned your finger." The child learned quickly and repeated through tears: "Yes, I hurt myself! I burned my finger!"

1.19 QUOTATION. "How? Can I point to the sensation? – Not in the usual sense. But I pronounce or write down the symbol and at the same time focus my attention on the sensation – I so to speak point to it in my mind. – But what is this ceremony good for? for it appears to be nothing else! The purpose of a definition is to determine the meaning of a symbol. – Well, it is done precisely by my focusing my attention; because by doing that, I impress the connection between the symbol and the sensation in my mind." (§258)

1.20 REMARK. There is no doubt that an association between a new feeling and a symbol can be established in just the way proposed by Wittgenstein's fictive partner of discussion and denied by Wittgenstein. When I was between 18 and 22 years old, I had at four occasions a strange feeling which I have otherwise not had, neither before nor after. When the feeling came, I was sitting at a table alone in a room and for a couple of minutes, a feeling of inner peace fell on my mind at the same time as the table and everything else in the room and in the world was felt to be far away. In this state, I asked myself, as an alarming and existentially important problem and not only as an academic question: "Why is there something and not rather nothing." I called the sensation "the remoteness feeling". In my mind, I connected this expression with the feeling in a kind of ostensive definition in just the way which Wittgenstein claims cannot be done. The expression got its meaning by the "ceremony". This worked perfectly well. The ceremony *was* good for something. For instance, I can say that I have not had the remoteness feeling since I was twenty-two, and altogether I have had it four times. Since what Wittgenstein claims to be impossible actually has been done, something is wrong about his opinion that expressions for sensations cannot refer to inner states. The further analysis must show what is wrong.

I consider a couple of objections to this example which I have encountered. One says that an expression in a private language is not allowed to contain any words from ordinary language. I am not convinced of the validity of this objection. Anyhow the example should work just as well if I had called the sensation "abracadabra" or "S". Another objection claims that one *can* give new names to inner sensations, but they do not belong to a language. The reason for this claim seems to be that such new expressions cannot be used to communicate with other people. This objection is not valid. A language can be used for several purposes other than communicating with other people. Some people write a diary only to support their own memory without ever intending anybody else than themselves to read it. Some people even write a diary without intending themselves to read it again. They write it just as a means to express their thoughts and in that way clarify them. Language can not only be used for interpersonal communication. Language can also be used for intrapersonal communication.

1.21 QUOTATION. "Well, it is done precisely by my focusing my attention; because by doing that, I impress the connection between the symbol and the sensation in my mind. – 'I impress it in my mind' can, however, only mean: this procedure brings about that I in the future remember the connection *correctly*. But in our case, I have no criterion of the correctness. Here one might say: correct is that which always appears correct to me. And that only means that here it is not possible to talk about 'correct'." (§258)

1.22 REMARK. The symbol "S" refers to a *type* of sensation. Therefore an understanding of the meaning of "S" must include a method for distinguishing such individual sensations which are of type S from those which are not. The method is a recursive decision algorithm associated with S. Such algorithms use to contain components which work automatically and therefore are unconscious. For a predicate like S, the decision method is the essential component in the meaning. Wittgenstein's demand is then that there must be a criterion for the correct association of "S" with the decision method. Since only I know about the connection, the criterion can only be the following: the information about the algorithm and its connection with "S" is stored in my memory at the occasion of the ostensive definition and after that, the information is unchanged and accessible to me, and the unconscious components of the algorithm work as required. As long as the criterion is satisfied *as a matter of fact*, this suffices for practical purposes, that is, for my own private use of the sign "S" in a correct way. Of course, it does not suffice for communicating with other persons about S; but since I write the diary about S only for my own private purposes, this does not matter. Wittgenstein's demand could be that a criterion of meaning must be intersubjective. Such a demand is justified in the case of an expression used for communication between individuals; it is anything but obvious if the expression is used only for private purposes of one person. Justified or not, the demand can in principle be satisfied even in the latter case. By examining the brain from outside, it is in principle possible for somebody else to verify or falsify that the information about the algorithm and its connection with "S" is unchanged in my memory and accessible to my mind whenever I want it and that the automatic components of the algorithm work properly.

1.23 QUOTATION. "What reason do we have for calling "S" the sign for a *sensation?* 'Sensation' is after all a word in our common language and not in a language intelligible only to me. The use of this word is in need of a justification which everybody will understand." (§261)

1.24 REMARK. There is a decision method for S, and there is a decision method for sensations in general. If the decision algorithm for sensations gives a positive output for a given input whenever the decision algorithm for S gives a positive output for the same input, then it is justified to call S a sensation. The situation is the same here as with many other pairs of predicates, including such predicates which are concerned only with phenomena in space and time.

1.25 ANALYSIS. It is useful also to analyse how words connected with perception get meaning. Suppose I want to teach a child U the meaning of the colour words "red", "green" etc. I take care that the appropriate external physical circumstances are present: objects of various colours are placed in a visible place in front of U and at a suitable distance; it is sufficiently bright and the light falling on the objects is white; there is nothing opaque between U's eyes and the objects, etc. I place a sequence of objects of different shades of red before the child and say for each object "This is a red object." I continue with a sequence of green objects of different nuances. After a while, U has understood the ostensive definitions and can himself with great certainty select what is red, what is green, and what is neither. U has understood the meaning of "red" and "green". This implies that he has associated one algorithm with the word "red" and another algorithm with the word "green". It is not important whether U's algorithms are the same as mine. What does matter is that they classify the same objects as red and the same objects as green as my algorithms do.

What is the criterion of redness in an algorithm used by human beings unaided by any apparatus? (Note that this is another sort of criteria than those wanted by Wittgenstein in §258.) It is fairly easy to build a robot which identifies the colour of an object. It measures the frequency of the light reflected from the surface of the object. If the bulk of the light beams have frequencies in the interval from 4.3×10^{14} Hz to 4.8×10^{14} Hz, then the object is classified by the robot as red. There are similar criteria for the other colours. The algorithm and the criteria used by a human being unaided by instruments are different. In particular, our criteria are not numerical. We distinguish colours by the phenomenological quality of the impression which the watching of a coloured object leaves in the mind. Red has one phenomenological character, green another. Such criteria are made possible by the self-awareness.

The kind of activity which U and I carry out in order that U should learn the meaning of the colour words is called a *language game* by Wittgenstein. I now try to analyse precisely what happens during such a language game. The algorithm associated with the colour word "red" gives the basic meaning of the word. Since I attach a meaning to the word "red", I have one such algorithm associated with "red". This includes the criterion for redness based on the phenomenological quality of the impression which a red object leaves in my mind. This reference to an inner, private state in me is part of the meaning I attach to "red"; but since it is inner, I cannot convey this part of the meaning to U during the language game. The part of the meaning of "red" which I can transfer to U is the extension of redness: which objects are red and which are not. U has understood the meaning of "red" when he has found or developed an algorithm which selects precisely the same objects as red as my algorithm does. U's algorithm also contains a criterion of redness based on the phenomenological qualities of red in his mind. His algorithm need not be the same as mine, and the phenomenological character of redness in his mind need not be the same as in mine. What is important is that the two algorithms give the same results on redness and non-redness. U's criterion of redness is part of the meaning which he attaches to "red". Thus also the meaning U attaches to "red" contains a reference to something internal and private in U's mind. Still U and I, and everybody else who use "red" in the same way as we do, can communicate on redness, and understand each other. (Incidentally, this shows that meaning and use are not the same.)

Does a person with an inverted colour spectrum associate another meaning with the word "red" than a normal person does? Yes! They have different criteria of redness. The criterion of redness is part of the meaning of "red". Therefore the meanings they attach to "red" must differ. This is no obstacle to communication between them. What matters in the interpersonal communication is that they use the word "red" in the same way, that is, that they classify the same objects as red with their different criteria and different meanings attached to "red".

It is easy to see that the meanings of words for pain and other sensations, in essentially the same way as colour words, contain a reference to inner, private states. Similarly, words for the other psychological phenomena listed in Thesis (12-1) contain references to inner states, processes, and events.

1.26 EXAMPLE. (I) We can make aesthetic judgements about colours: "Green is beautiful." "Red is pleasant. I enjoy red." "Red and green match each other well." We consider the example:

(26-1)   Red is pleasant. I enjoy red.

Such a judgement presupposes self-awareness. By saying so, I express how I react to the phenomenological character of red. The statement is intelligible to anybody who knows that I am self-aware and that the meaning I attach to "red" contains a reference to the phenomenological character that red has to me (whatever it may be). The semantic ideas in Analysis 1.25 make aesthetic judgements intelligible.

(II) A dream is a mental process occurring during sleep and which produces images deceptively similar to the images produced by watching a real scenery.

Children learn quite early on in their lives to distinguish dreams from perceptions. Dreams are like perceptions except that they are not caused by any external scenery. Therefore both "dreaming" and "perceiving" have in their meanings a reference to the existence of an inner process. "Dream (content)" and "perception (content)" have in their meanings a reference to the existence of inner images.

1.27 EXAMPLE. Suppose a person P is colour-blind. This is a handicap, not least in the traffic. To reduce his handicap, P buys an optical instrument which can discern colours. The device works, as described in Analysis 1.25, by measuring wave frequencies and using numerical criteria for the colours. When an analysis has been made, the instrument gives the colour of a surface it has been exposed to via a display where the user of the instrument can read the colour of the surface scrutinised: 'red', 'green', or whatever it is. Using the device, P can classify objects according to colour with about the same certainty as a person with full colour seeing who uses only his unaided eye and the phenomenological criteria. Still P will not be able to understand aesthetic judgements about colours. This shows that the hypothesis about the existence of an inner image of, for instance, red in other people and the existence of phenomenological qualities in such an image is part of the full meaning of the word "red". Such an existence hypothesis is an anthropological hypothesis. Thus an empirical, anthropological hypothesis can be part of the fully developed meaning of a colour word. It also shows how a reference to something inner can be part of the meaning of a colour word. This part of the meaning does not affect all uses of colour words, for instance not when we classify objects according to colour; but it does affect the use of colour words in aesthetic judgements.

1.28 QUOTATION. "If I say about myself that I only know from my own case what the word 'pain' means, – don't I have to say the same about other people too? And how can I then generalise this one single case in such an irresponsible manner? Nevertheless everybody says about himself that he only knows from himself what pain is!" (§293)

1.29 REMARK. Analysis 1.25 shows that I only know from myself the *full* meaning of the word "pain", in agreement with the common view; and it *is* the same with other people. The generalisation is, however, not irresponsible. It is based on the very reasonable and well-founded empirical hypothesis that human beings are composed and function in mainly the same way (as I do). Analysis 1.25 shows that all we need to assume is that other people are self-aware and decide the extensions of concepts for colours and sensations by algorithms which are built into the organism itself and have a criterion for the output which is immediately accessible to the person's consciousness.

In my philosophy, the common sense opinion, that everybody only knows from himself what pain is, is correct. Analysis 1.25 shows that the meaning of "red" has two dimensions: the extension of redness and the inner, phenomenological character of redness. Similarly, the meaning of "pain" has two dimensions: the extension of pain and the inner, phenomenological character of pain. The extension of pain can be decided by external, for instance medical, criteria. But only a person who has himself suffered pain can understand the full meaning of the word "pain". Most of us experience only quite easy pain in life. Some forms of cancer are known to give very intense and permanent pain which places an enormous physical and psychological strain on the patient. A person who has gone trough such an ordeal can truly say that this experience has given the meaning of the word "pain" a new dimension.

1.30 QUOTATION. "Suppose that everyone had a box in which there were something called 'a beetle'. No one is ever able to look into another person's box; and everybody says that he knows only from the sight of his own beetle what a beetle is. – Then it might be possible that everybody had a different thing than the others. In fact, one might even imagine that such a thing is in constant change. – But if, in spite of that, these people still had a use for the word 'beetle'? – In that case, it would not be a designation for a thing. The thing in the box does not at all belong to the language game, not even as a *something:* because the box might even be empty. – Indeed, this thing in the box can be 'reduced'; it disappears from the picture whatever its nature may have been.

In other words: If we construct the grammar of the expression for a sensation according to the model 'object and name', then the object slips out of consideration as irrelevant." (§293)

1.31 REMARK. Refer to Analysis 1.25 and think of the boxes as U's mind and my mind and the beetles as the image of red in U's mind and the image of red in my mind. Then it is, indeed, possible that the two images are different. As a matter of fact, it is probable that they are not completely similar. It is even possible that the images change over time. Also this is actually quite probable because there are good reasons to believe they are not exactly the same over a whole lifetime. This is of no importance as long as the algorithms, in which the images have a role, distinguish in the same way between red and non-red objects. Analysis 1.25 shows that the character of the image of red has no role in the language game for "red" played by U and me, just as claimed by Wittgenstein. But he is wrong in concluding that then it has no place in the meaning of "red" either. In contrast to what Wittgenstein's erroneously believes, the meaning of words like "red", "green", "pain" and "sensation" is not completely determined by the language game as the example in Analysis 1.25 clearly shows. The "beetle in the box", that is, the reference to the inner state, also contributes to the meaning as explained in Remark 1.29. Therefore "the thing in the box *cannot* be reduced." Wittgenstein is wrong in his claim that "the box might also be empty." For a predicate like "red", U *must* have an algorithm for the extension of redness; and U's image of redness is part of his algorithm. That image is in Wittgenstein's analogy "the beetle in the box". The same obtains for predicates like "pain" and "sensation".

1.32 REMARK. Other philosophers, for instance Michael Dummett, have given support to Thesis (10-1): Everything that affects the meaning of expressions in a public language like English must be something which is itself public and knowable by anyone. In particular, the meaning of such expressions cannot contain any reference to private mental states, processes, and events of the sort discussed above. I briefly comment on two arguments from this post-Wittgensteinian literature.

1.33 **The Acquisition Argument.** Suppose L is a public language containing an expression "E" whose meaning depends on the nature of certain private states in competent speakers. Let U be a person learning the language L and in particular acquiring an understanding of the expression "E". Then U must come to use it in connection with his own private states of the same kind as those associated with "E" by the competent speakers. But since these states (in the competent speakers) are private, they are not accessible to U, so how can U identify the right state in himself to associate with "E"?

1.34 REMARK. The argument rests on the assumption that meaning is use. If the meaning of "E" is identical with the use of "E", then the problem pointed out in the acquisition argument does arise. But as mentioned in Analysis 1.25, meaning cannot be identified with use. It is useful to consider two examples.

(I) In Analysis 1.25, we considered an example where I teach U the meaning of the colour words. The meaning of the predicate "red" for me is the algorithm I associate with the word. I teach U the meaning of "red" by helping him to find or develop a suitable algorithm to associate with the word "red". It need not be the same algorithm as mine and, in particular, the output state in U's mind of the algorithm, the colour image, need not be the same as mine. What is required is that the two algorithms assign the same extension to "red". When this is satisfied, U and I use the word "red" in the same way. We see that the meaning of the word "red" has two components. One component is the extension. It is public and can be identified with the use. It is the same for all users. The other component is private. It consists of the algorithm for the extension of "red" and notably the inner state which in the mind is conceived of as the image of redness. It may vary from individual to individual as long as it gives the same output to the question about what is red and what is not. The question in the acquisition argument is: How can U identify the right state in himself to associate with "red"? The answer is that there is no *the* right state. U must just find *some* algorithm and *some* state which assigns the same extension to "red" as my algorithm and state do and as any other competent speaker's algorithm and state do.

(II) The second example is the aesthetic judgement "Red is pleasant. I enjoy red" from Example 1.26. It presupposes self-awareness in the speaker. The speaker V expresses how he reacts to the phenomenological qualities of his inner image of red. For a listener U to understand the statement, U must assume that there exists an inner image of red in V and that the image has some phenomenological qualities. These existence conditions, he can infer from his belief that V, and most other human beings, are quite similar to himself. For the understanding, he needs, however, know nothing about just what the image is and what phenomenological qualities it has. Suppose U learns from V and also wants to make an aesthetic statement, for instance "I must admit that I am not very fond of red. It makes me sad." Here there is a right state for U to identify, namely the one he learned from me to associate with the word "red". But it need not be the same state that V has associated with the word "red". U's judgement on how he reacts to the phenomenological qualities of red must be based on just that state which he himself has associated with "red" when he learned the meaning of "red". All V needs in order to understand U's judgement is again the existence condition that there exists an inner image of red in U and that the image has some phenomenological qualities.

1.35 **The Manifestation Argument.** This argument views the process from the teacher's side. How can the teacher know that the learner U has associated the right meaning with the expression "E"? To grasp the right meaning is to connect a particular private state rather than others with "E". Because the states in U are private, it is impossible for the teacher to check that U has associated the right inner state with "E" and it is impossible for U to manifest the association.

1.36 REMARK. To understand the meaning of an expression is *not* to associate one particular meaning with the expression, the same meaning as the teacher. It is to associate some meaning with the expression, a meaning which determines the same use of the expression as the teacher's use. Again the example in Analysis 1.25 is useful.

When U learns the colours from me, the meaning eventually attached to "red" by U is determined by the algorithm, including his image of red, which he uses to determine the extension of the predicate "red". The meaning *I* associate with "red" is determined by *my* extension algorithm and *my* image of red. U's algorithm and U's image of red may well be different from mine. Then the meaning U associates with "red" is different from the meaning I associate with "red". For U to have understood the meaning of "red", his algorithm must yield the same result on which objects are red and which are not as my algorithm does. This can easily be checked by the teacher. When this is satisfied, U and I use, in the given context, the word "red" in the same way. This is perfectly compatible with the possibility that the private components of the meanings which U and I assign to "red" are different.

1.37 CONCLUSION. Wittgenstein's first thesis states that there is no private language, that is, there is no language which can only be understood by its single user but which cannot, even in principle, be understood by anybody else. The thesis is correct; but Wittgenstein's argument for it is erroneous.

Wittgenstein's second thesis states that expressions concerned with sensations do not in their meanings contain a reference to inner, private states. This thesis is false. The arguments advanced by Wittgenstein and Dummett are insufficient and erroneous. The meaning of a colour word can be identified with the criterion by which we distinguish that colour from other colours and other phenomena, namely the phenomenological qualities of that colour in the mind. Similarly the meaning of a word for a sensation can be identified with the criterion – based on the inner, phenomenological qualities – by which we distinguish that sensation from other sensations and other phenomena. The exact character of these phenomenological qualities plays no role in the use of the words; but in aesthetic judgements, the *existence* of the phenomenological qualities is essential.

2. Meaning

2.1 Introduction. Maybe the best known statement in the philosophy of the later Wittgenstein is:

(1-1)   *Meaning is essentially use.*

This is Wittgenstein's meaning theory. The following quotation gives another formulation of the idea: "For a large class of cases – though not for all – in which we employ the word 'meaning', it can be defined thus: the meaning of a word is its use in the language." (§43)

(1-2)   *The meaning of a word is its use in the language.*

2.2 REMARK. A question to consider is the interpretation of the statements. First: What does "essentially" mean here? I will take it to mean that *fundamentally* and *primarily*, meaning is use (in the language). Occasionally one hears or reads uses of words which do not agree with their ordinary use in the language. To the extent in which such uses are intelligible, they are secondary and derived. For example, when Franz Kafka was dying in cancer and suffered severe pain, he is reported to have said to his friend Max Brodd: "If you don't kill me, then you are a murderer!" Here Kafka uses the word "murderer" in a way in which it is not used in ordinary language. Nevertheless the statement is completely intelligible. It is a metaphorical way of saying: "If you don't relieve me of this terrible pain (which can only be done by killing me), then you commit a (moral) crime at the level of murder." It shows that Kafka has used "murderer" in a secondary sense which is parasitic on its common and primary meaning.

Second: What can Wittgenstein's motives for identifying meaning with use be? The answer is implicit in the private language argument. This argument is meant to support Wittgenstein's thesis that no word in the public language can in its meaning have a reference to an inner state or process. Therefore the word "meaning", in particular, does not in its meaning have a reference to something which is psychologically inward. Then only the public and outward *use* of a word is left to identify its meaning with: Meaning *is* use. Thus Wittgenstein's theory of meaning is really just a corollary to the private language argument.

One consequence of Wittgenstein's definition of meaning is that the meaning of a word or expression cannot exist independently of and before the word or expression. Formulated as a slogan (my own formulation, not Wittgenstein's):

(2-1)   *No meaning without language.*

In the present section, I will argue the following theses in opposition to Wittgenstein's views:

(2-2)   *Meaning can be identified with something that is on a self-conscious individual's mind. Meaning determines use but cannot be identified with use.*

(2-3)   *Language is an instrument for the expression of meanings.*

(2-4)   *Meaning precedes ontologically and temporarily language. Thus meaning can exist prior to and independently of language.*

Again these ideas coincide with the primitive common sense views of the man in the street as opposed to Wittgenstein's sophisticated philosophical standpoint.

2.3 ANALYSIS. Since Wittgenstein's theory of meaning is a corollary to the private language argument and this argument is invalid, it might be possible that even the theory of meaning is invalid. Since words for colours and sensations in their meanings contain a reference to a psychologically inner state, it might be that even the word "meaning" does so. It might even be that meaning can be identified with something inner.

It is useful to consider how the word "red" gets its meaning. The eyes and the central nervous system contain a mechanism for seeing. Most of the mechanism works without its possessor being conscious of how it works. A mechanism is essentially the same as an algorithm. One part of the algorithm may become conscious, namely the final result of the working of the algorithm: the image. We can discern three aspects of the attribution of meaning to the word "red".

(1) *The phenomenological qualities of the image of red.* They are the criterion by which we distinguish red from non-red. Such a criterion *must* be part of the meaning of "red". The image and its phenomenological qualities are inner and private in the psychological sense. We call the image and its phenomenological qualities for *private meaning.* Since we, and other self-aware animals, can be conscious of redness and its distinguishing criterion before we learn any word for redness, private meaning is ontologically prior to language.

(2) *The association of the word "red" with its private meaning.* Such an association is, in the present example, brought about by a learning process based on an ostensive definition. It is part of the definition of the recursive semantic function F introduced in Analysis 1.6. For some words there are other ways than ostensive definitions to learn their meaning, for example explicit or contextual definitions.

(3) *The use of the word "red".* The association of a word with its private meaning determines the use of the word. The association gives the *rule* for the use of "red". In the examples in Section 1, we found two types of uses. In a *first-order use*, the criterion of redness is applied but not referred to. First-order uses occur in the labelling of objects as red or non-red. In a *second-order use*, there is an implicit reference to the existence of the phenomenological qualities of redness. Aesthetic statements on redness are examples of second-order uses of "red". The use of a word is the public reflection of the private meaning. We may call use a *public representation of meaning.*

Private meaning, together with the rule for the association of a word with its private meaning, determines the use. Use does not determine private meaning. As shown in Analysis 1.25, one and the same use of "red" is compatible with more than one algorithm for redness. In particular, it is compatible with more than one criterion of redness (which is the private meaning). Therefore private meaning *is* meaning. Meaning is prior to language and language is an instrument for the expression of meaning, as claimed in theses (2-3) and (2-4). Meaning is not primarily use.

Language is used to express meanings. It is not used to express use in the language. Therefore meaning is not use in the language. Language is normally used to communicate what is on a person's mind. Therefore meaning is normally identical with something that is on a person's mind.

2.4 IDEA. When I first some years ago heard that chimpanzees (or, more precisely, bonobos) can learn to speak (a fragment of) a human language, I immediately connected it with the well-known fact that chimpanzees are self-aware and self-conscious. This gave the first hypothesis:

(4-1)   *Self-awareness is a necessary condition for meaning.*

The next idea came immediately after:

(4-2)   *Self-awareness is a sufficient condition for meaning.*

Here are a couple of reasons for believing in Thesis (4-1). No animal is known who can understand an essential fragment of a language, that is, phrases and sentences beyond simple commands, without having self-awareness. To mean something, a being must be able to intend to communicate the meaning to another being which is not possible without self-awareness. For Thesis (4-2), we consider perception. If a self-conscious individual sees a scene and is aware of his seeing the scene, then the scene is on his mind. Then it is something he, in principle, can want to communicate to another individual, that is, a meaning. A similar case can be made for thoughts, fantasies, memories, ideas, and intentions. This leads to the following thesis.

(4-3)   *The meaning of a sentence is what the speaker wants to communicate by the sentence. Normally this coincides with something in the speaker's consciousness.*

Thus meanings exist in all self-aware beings: human beings, chimpanzees, bonobos, orangutangs, gorillas, dolphins, and elephants. Language arises much later in the evolution, as an instrument for the communication of content of consciousness. It took a considerable evolutionary pressure to develop an efficient instrument for communication of the contents of mind: language. Though some earlier human species, like the Homo Neanderthalis, no doubt were able to speak, really complex languages seem to have arisen only with Homo Sapiens Sapiens.

2.5 OBJECTION. When we see a red object, it is the object itself we see and not the image of it. Then also the criterion of redness must be connected with the object itself and not with the image of it.

REPLY:
When we see a red object, a mechanism which involves the eyes and parts of the brain is active. The perception creates a state in the brain which is immediately accessible to our consciousness. The consciousness has no direct access to the object. Therefore the basic criterion of redness can only be in terms of the inner state. An automatic projection operation then projects the redness out on the external object. The existence of such a projection operation can be proven by a simple experiment. It was communicated to me and the rest of the class by the biology teacher in secondary school, miss Rigmor Holt. Take a peg! Hold one end of it firmly in the hand! Move the other end over an uneven surface! When we thus use the peg as a tool, we feel an unevenness which we automatically locate to that end of the peg which is in contact with the surface. We certainly do not feel the unevenness directly because there are no nerves in the peg. What we do feel directly are the vibrations in that end of the peg which we hold in the hand. They are the basic criterion of unevenness. By an automatic projection, we then locate and feel the unevenness of the surface at the other end of the peg. (If we hold the peg only with a loose grip, the automatic projection disappears and we feel only the vibrations in that end of the peg which we hold in the hand. Now the peg is no longer used as a tool and as a prolongation of the arm and hand.) The case with the perception of the red object is similar. We are directly aware of the state in the brain. The basic criterion of redness must be formulated in terms of it. But by the automatic miss Holt projection function, we assign redness to the external object, and we do, indeed, see the object as red and not the image as red. In the same way, many other things we have in mind can be and are projected out in the external world.

2.6 OBJECTION. The identification of meaning with something that is on an individual's mind makes meaning psychologically internal. Meaning can be communicated, while something inner cannot. Therefore this theory of meaning must be false and the private language argument be right after all.

REPLY:
Our criterion of redness is the phenomenological character of the colour. It is something inner. The criterion of redness *must* be part of the meaning of the word "red" which therefore contains a reference to something psychologically internal. The objection can therefore not be correct. The problem here is to

show how meaning being internal is compatible with the communicability of meaning.

First consider the predicate "red". Its meaning is determined by the algorithm used to distinguish red objects from non-red objects and, in particular, the criterion of redness in the algorithm. Let us say that two algorithms are *equivalent* if they always give the same output for the same input. Suppose I and another speaker U both have learned the meaning of "red". Then our algorithms and criteria of redness need not be identical. If so, the private meanings we assign to "red" are not identical. However, our algorithms and criteria of redness must be equivalent. If they are equivalent, we use "red" in the same way. Thus two speakers can use a word or a phrase in the same way and still assign different (private) meanings to it. One individual V can teach another individual U the use of the word "red"; but he cannot teach U the meaning of "red". U himself supplies an algorithm and a criterion for redness which fit the use. Then and only then does U assign a meaning to "red". The meaning is not uniquely determined by the use; but for U, the meaning determines the use.

Suppose I watch an object G and see that it is red. I inform U of this by the sentence

(6-1)   Object G is red.

We assume that U knows which object is named by "G". By the theory of meaning in (2-2), the meaning of the sentence (6-1) is what is on my mind. By the projection function, what is on my mind is an external state of affairs, a fact. The fact can be formulated as follows:

(6-2)   If an individual applies his visual algorithm for redness to object G and his algorithm is equivalent with mine, then the outcome will be affirmative.

A fact is determined by its verification algorithm. Facts are not in general what true statements state. Because of the effect of the projection function, the formulation (6-2) gives a public representation of the meaning of the declarative sentence (6-1) rather than the meaning itself. We see that the private meaning of "red" does not occur in the public meaning representation of "Object G is red" because (6-2) only demands equivalence of the algorithms, not identity. Speaker and hearer communicate by public representations of meaning. Each understands the message by supplying his own private meanings to the predicate "red". When we generalise this insight, we get the following results:

(6-3)   *The meanings of words and phrases are primarily private.*

(6-4)   *The meaning of a word or phrase occurring in a sentence does not enter into the public representation of the meaning of the sentence – be it declarative, interrogative, commanding or whatever. What does enter into the public representation of the meaning of the sentence is the public representation of the meaning of the word or phrase. It only demands equivalence, not necessarily identity, of the algorithms associated with the word or phrase, and therefore it only demands the same use, not necessarily the same meaning, of the expression. Speaker and hearer each supplies his own meaning to the expression. This makes communication by means of sentences possible.*

(6-5)   *We communicate with each other only by sentences and not by single words and phrases.*

I now apply the theory of meaning developed in the present section to some questions in the philosophy of language.

2.7 Thinking and language. What is the meaning of words like "thinking" and "thought"? According to the private language argument, they cannot refer to something inner. The criterion of the presence of a thought and thinking must be something outward. We might imagine that the outward phenomenon is a tendency to some type of movement. A trouble with this idea is that the movements are often not sufficiently specific to identify a thought uniquely. Suppose I think that I play football on Wembley Stadium in London. Then there might be a tendency to movements in my legs and body associated with running and kicking from which it might be possible to infer that I think about playing football; but it should be impossible from the movements to infer that I think about the playing taking place on Wembley. An alternative outward criterion of thinking which avoids this objection could instead be (silent) talking to oneself. Several followers of Wittgenstein and the Oxford philosophers have identified thinking with silent talking to oneself.

2.8 REMARK. An empirically based objection to this idea is that some animals without language, like wild chimpanzees, clearly can think and solve problems. The thesis in §2.7 is a consequence of the private language argument. In Section 1, the private language argument was rejected. Then we need not accept its consequences either. A consequence of the thesis in §2.7 is that all thoughts can be expressed in one or more sentences. Consider a thought expressed in a sentence p. Clearly the thought should be identified with the meaning of p rather than with p itself because the thought can be expressed by several different sentences if only they have the same meaning. But, as we have seen, meanings can exist before language. Therefore also thoughts can exist before language.

Thinking can be identified with problem solving. It is fairly easy to give examples of thinking which is not linguistic. Simple mechanical problems can be solved without being formulated in a language. Such problems are constantly solved by chimpanzees, both in captivity and in the wild. All that is needed is an ability to *perceive* the relevant mechanical system and to *imagine* the change in and manipulation of the system which solves the problem. Similarly some social problems can be solved without ever being formulated in any language. Via the self-consciousness, which implies an awareness that even other individuals of our species are self-conscious, and a hermeneutic method, many a psychological and social problem in a group can be solved without language being involved. Even in human beings with full linguistic competence, much thinking is non-linguistic. This is the case with thinking based on silent knowledge. Much of an artisan's competence is of this silent sort. Therefore also much of his thinking during his work is non-linguistic. If our thinking were exclusively in terms of words, figures in textbooks should not be needed. They should not the least help the reader in the understanding of the text. The term "image" here includes all kinds of impressions associated with the senses, for instance visual, auditory, and tactile images. Much of a composer's thinking is in terms of auditory images.

On the other hand, it is clear that a large part of our thinking does consist in silently speaking to ourselves. And the possibility of thoughts formulated in a language enormously increases our capacity for thinking. Clothing our thoughts into words makes it possible for us to think abstractly. Expressing thoughts in sentences makes it possible for us to construct long chains of reasoning and construct theories and other comprehensive systems of thoughts far beyond anything which is possible in wordless thinking. Einstein is reported to have said "My pen is smarter than I am" meaning that Einstein with a pen and paper is more than twice as smart as Einstein without these utilities. Similarly, Wittgenstein could have said "My language is smarter than I am" meaning that Wittgenstein with a language is more than twice as smart as Wittgenstein without it. But there is a large and unbridgeable gap between this and the conclusion that all thinking is linguistic. Most of our intellectual activity is a combination of thinking in terms of images and thinking in terms of words.

2.9 **Universal grammar.** Chomsky has tried to explain the amazing ease with which children learn their native tongue by postulating the existence of a *Universal Grammar* containing features which are common to all natural languages. The knowledge of the universal grammar is inborn in human beings. This knowledge is claimed to be domain-specific by being effective for the peculiar matter of language learning.

2.10 REMARK. Chomsky's ideas are not compatible with the theory of meaning stated above. Meaning is conscious content of the mind. Meanings precede sentences. Sentences are instruments for the expression of meanings. Whatever is common in all grammars should come from the meanings alone. But meaning, being the content of mind, is in itself non-linguistic. Therefore, if anything is universal in the grammars of natural languages, it cannot be language specific.

Chomsky nevertheless has a partly correct intuition. We first consider the simplest languages which are sufficient for the expression of all declarative sentences about the world, the languages of predicate logic. Their non-logical symbols fall in three categories: (1) constants, (2) predicates, and (3) function symbols. The corresponding ontology consists of: (1) individuals (named by constants), (2) properties and relations (named by predicates), and (3) functional relations (named by function symbols). These are the ontological categories which are used in the perception of the world. We see the world as a collection of individuals. We characterise the individuals by the properties they have and the relations which hold between them. We understand the working of systems by the functional relations obtaining between the parts. This is how our minds work at the most basic level. It gives rise to a non-linguistic syntax. For instance, we perceive that an individual a has a property P (in predicate logical languages often expressed as $P(a)$). Therefore the subject-predicate structure of a grammar is, indeed, inborn in human beings. But it is part of our innate cognitive faculty and is not language-specific. The same subject-predicate structure is innate in other self-aware, languageless beings who see the world essentially as we do, like for instance chimpanzees. What is needed for the child is to learn exactly how the subject-predicate structure is represented and expressed in the natural language he or she is learning. In English, to take an example, the grammatical subject cannot be omitted. Speakers of English say for instance:

> I am; you are; he, she, it is human; etc.

In Spanish, the grammatical subject is mostly omitted and is implicit in the verb-form or the context:

> Soy; eras; es humano; etc.

A predicate logical language also contains logical symbols like variables, quantifiers, and connectives. They also represent simple modes of functioning of the conscious mind. Thus 'A or B' is an exhaustive and exclusive list of alternative solutions to a problem which an individual with some imagination and analytical ability can produce. 'If A then B' represents a functional connection between an input event described by A and an output event described by B which an individual with a sufficient understanding of the functional connection can intuit. A predicate logical language gets closer to natural languages in expressive power by being enriched with further expressive options like tenses, interrogatives, modalities, and expressions for propositional attitudes. They also represent pre-linguistic function modes of the mind. Thus tenses express the mind's ordering of events and actions in time. Propositional attitudes like 'I know that A' and 'he believes that B' are implicit in the self-consciousness of the mind, including the awareness that even other human beings are self-aware.

To sum up: There is, indeed, a kind of innate Universal Grammar. It pertains, however, to our general cognitive faculty and is not, in contrast to Chomsky's claim, language-specific. The fact that meanings and cognition-based syntactic structures are present in our minds before we start to learn our first language partly explains the ease with which young children learn the language. The other part of the explanation is that children and young persons have an innate appetite for and ability to learn and remember a large number of words and grammatical combinations and connect them with meanings and situations. It is not clear whether that ability is language-specific because young children also have an innate appetite for and ability to adapt to their non-linguistic physical and social environment.

2.11 **Language of thought.** A common idea among psychologists and philosophers is that the brain (and mind) is a Turing machine. Its essential cognitive activity, including thinking, must therefore consist in computations. This has led some philosophers, for instance Harman and Fodor, to the hypothesis of a *language of thought* by the following sequence of reasoning.

Computations presuppose representations. Thus computations of a Turing machine or a computer are often defined over numerals that represent numbers. The suggestion is then that the sort of computations in the brain which are thinking requires the kind of representations which are normally used for thoughts, namely sentences. The language of thought is a formal language encoded in the brains of human beings (and possibly other intelligent creatures) as a vehicle for their thoughts. The claim is that thinking consists in performing computations on sentences belonging to this language of thought (which is innate). Inferences in this language are unconscious causal processes.

2.12 REMARK. The language of thought hypothesis is not compatible with the picture of language exposed in the present section. This picture explicitly presupposes that there is thinking which is not represented in any language. An analysis reveals what is wrong in the chain of reasoning that leads to the language of thought hypothesis. A computation is a physical process. It operates on physical states. Thus a computation in a computer operates on electronic marks. To interpret the physical process as a computation, the physical states must be taken as representations of something else. Thinking consists in computations on physical states in the brain. These brain states can be, but need not be, interpreted as representing sentences. In the case of thinking about a mechanical problem, for instance, they can be interpreted as representing images of states in the mechanical system under consideration. Much human thinking is in terms of images which do not represent sentences. Therefore the language of thought hypothesis is false. Some thinking is non-linguistic and in terms of images. Some thinking is linguistic and consists of silently talking to oneself. Only in the latter case is there a language of thought, the natural language in terms of which we think. It is the only kind of language of thought there is.

One part of the language of thought hypothesis states that the language of thought obeys a logic similar to predicate logic. The brain is so constructed, it is claimed, that if it is in a state which represents the premises (represented in the language of thought), then it is sometimes caused to enter a state which represents the conclusion. Thus, in the case of the language of thought, inference is a *causal* process. This causal logic is a consequence of the way the brain is constructed and therefore is innate. However, empirical investigations show that there is no innate logic in human beings. We *must* have a logic in order to solve problems and therefore all normal grown-up humans have a logic. But strong empirical evidence suggests that we acquire our logical competence in the same way in which we get other vital skills: by adapting to the environment in which we grow up and live. The Russian psychologist A. R. Luria made in the 1930s investigations of the reasoning ability of peasants in Kirghizia and Uzbekistan. His purpose was to clarify the role of literacy in the logical competence of people. Here is an interview with an illiterate Uzbek villager. Q is the interviewer and P the peasant.

Q: "In the far north where there is snow, all bears are white. Novaya Zemla is in the far north, and there is always snow there. What colours are the bears there?"

P: "There are different sorts of bears. [The syllogism was repeated.] I do not know. I have seen a black bear; I have never seen any others... Each locality has its own animals: if it is white, they will be white; if it is yellow, they will be yellow."

Q: "But what kind of bears are there in Novaya Zemla?"

P: "We always speak of what we see; we do not talk about what we have not seen."

Q: "But what do my words imply?" [The syllogism was repeated.]

P: "Well, it is like this: our tsar is not like yours, and yours is not like ours. Your words can be answered only by someone who was there, and if a person was not there, he cannot say anything on the basis of your words."

Q: "But on the basis of my words, 'in the north, where the bears are white', can you gather what kind of bears there are in Novaya Zemla?"

P: "If a man was sixty or eighty and had seen a white bear and had told about it, he could be believed, but I have never seen one and hence I cannot say anything!" [At this point, a young Uzbek volunteered: "From your words, it means that the bears there are white."]

Q: "Who of you is right?"
P: "What the cock knows how to do, he does. What I know, I say, and nothing beyond that!"

The peasant shows great intellectual integrity. He expresses the consequences of a purely empirical methodology. Suppose a modern, western researcher has detected a certain frequency of a medical phenomenon in a large group of white, Caucasian men. If asked "How is it with white, Caucasian women?", he might answer, in the same vein as the Uzbek peasant, "I don't know; we have not examined it." To the question "How is the frequency among Asians and Africans?", the researcher's answer should be the same "I don't know; we have not examined it." (Compare with the peasant's declaration: "We always speak of what we see; we do not talk about what we have not seen.") Everybody, including an elderly Uzbek peasant in the 1930s, needs a logic. Otherwise thinking and problem solving become impossible. Peasant P's answers to the interviewer Q show that his logic is empirical, and not a post-Aristotelian theoretical logic. Had the peasant had an inborn logic of thought akin to the usual predicate logic, he should immediately have given the answer which the post-Aristotelian interviewer expected.

2.13 **Meaning and intention.** It is felt intuitively that there is a close relation between meaning, intention, and communication. In an article from 1957, Paul Grice has tried to analyse meaning in terms of intention and communication. His contention is that basically and primarily, "a person M meant such-and-such by the sentence p" is equivalent with "M uttered p with the intention of inducing a belief to the effect that such-and-such by means of the recognition of this intention". Thus, according to Grice, successful communication, that is, the attainment of adequate understanding in a hearer H, requires recognition from the hearer of the speaker's intention in the communication process. It seems clear that he identifies the meaning of p with this intention.

2.14 REMARK. (I) No doubt meaning can be identified with intention in some contexts. Thus the meaning of an action is what is intended by it. But the meaning of a sentence cannot be identified with intention in the way Grice does. It is useful here to invoke the distinction between act and content. Meaning cannot be identified with an act of intending because the meaning of a sentence clearly is not an act; but neither can it be identified with the content of the intention. The content of the intention – that is, what is intended – is the induction of "a belief to the effect that such-and-such by means of the recognition of this intention". But this cannot be identified with the meaning of the sentence p either because meaning precedes ontologically the sentence and any speech act in which it may occur.

(II) The meaning of p is rather the content of p which M tries to (intends to) communicate. It is *normally* identical with something which is on M's conscious mind and which he tries to transfer to the mind of another conscious individual in the situation considered in Grice's definition. Thus the meaning is the content which M wants to communicate and not the content of the intention itself. Grice's analysis of meaning can therefore not be valid.

As an example, consider the following situation. I am known as a notorious liar. Even U knows that I am a notorious liar, and I know that U considers me a completely unreliable person. It is true that p, but I want to make U believe that $\neg p$. I therefore tell U that p. As I expect, U reacts according to his opinion on me: "That man is a consistent liar. He should never inform me that p if p were true. Therefore $\neg p$ must be the case." What I intend by uttering p is to induce the belief that $\neg p$ in U and not to induce the belief that p; but the intention to induce the belief that $\neg p$ is certainly not the meaning of p.

(III) If Grice does not analyse the meaning of p, what does he analyse? He analyses the meaning of an action, namely the speech act of uttering p. One objection to this is that the meaning of p is such-and-such while the meaning of the speech act, in the normal case, is to induce the belief that such-and-such. They are not identical. In my analysis, the meaning of p is the content of p that such-and-such and not the intention to induce the belief that such-and-such. Another objection is that meaning logically and ontologically is more fundamental than any speech act and therefore should not be defined in terms of speech acts.

(IV) To motivate the qualification "normally" in Part (II) above, it is instructive to look at the case of lying. Suppose M utters p and is lying. Then M is not communicating what is on his mind. Rather he communicates what he pretends to be on his mind. Thus in this case, the meaning of p is not identical with what is on M's mind but what he pretends to be on his mind. We therefore get:

(14-1) *Primarily, when the speaker is sincere, the meaning of an uttered sentence is something which is on the speaker's mind and which he intends to communicate.*

(14-2) *Secondarily, when the speaker is not sincere (for instance in the case of lying or acting), the meaning of an uttered sentence is something which the speaker pretends to be on his mind and which he intends to communicate.*

Consequently, in my semantic theory,

(14-3) *The meaning of p is what is communicated by p, and in the normal and primary case, this is something that is on the speaker's mind.*

2.15 **Rule-following.** Wittgenstein's view is that a word or expression is used correctly if it is used in accordance with a rule. The rule associates the expression with its meaning. This is in agreement with the ideas defended in the present essay. The difference lies in the definition of meaning. For Wittgenstein, meaning is use in the language. Therefore a Wittgensteinian rule associates a word or other expression with the set of language-games that is its meaning.

2.16 REMARK. The first objection to Wittgenstein's idea of a semantic rule is that it should put superhuman demands on the human memory. Each grown-up person knows several thousands of words and expressions. If each of them is associated with a whole set of situations together with information about how to use the expression in each situation, then the rule associated with the expression becomes quite complicated. Adding the complexities for all the thousands of words and expressions we know results in a body of knowledge beyond at least the capacity of my small head. Taking into consideration that some of us know several languages, the weight placed on the memory becomes unbearable. Thus I, to take a nearby example, speak three languages fluently and two more fairly well and some people speak more than five languages.

Another objection is the following. When I look introspectively into my own mind to see how I associate a word like "red" with its meaning, the following picture emerges. I know the phenomenological qualities of different nuances of red. The simple semantic rule I follow consists in the association of the phenomenological qualities of redness with the word "red". Such a rule is easy to remember. The situations and language-games by which I once upon a time learned which meaning to associate with "red" are long forgotten. They are pedagogical means to the learning of the meaning of the word, not the meaning itself.

To sum up: If meaning had been use, most of us should be able to learn only a rather small fragment of a natural language. Fortunately, meaning is not use, except for a few special expressions, and we are able to master not only one but several languages of several thousands of words and expressions and different grammars.

2.17 Kripke on rule-following. Ostensive definitions are definitions taught by means of examples. Thus we learn the rule for the use of an expression by being confronted with a finite selection of examples of the use of the rule. Kripke claims that there is a major problem with this kind of definitions. Suppose I am being taught a rule (a recursive function) a_i by being informed about the first four values 2, 4, 6, 8. Thus I am informed that

(17-1) $a_0 = 2, a_1 = 4, a_2 = 6, a_3 = 8$

The trouble is that there are infinitely many ways of continuing the sequence. They give rise to infinitely many recursive functions, for instance corresponding to sequences with initial segments

(17-2)   2, 4, 6, 8, 10, 12, 14, 16, ...

(17-3)   2, 4, 6, 8, 11, 15, 20, 26, ...

(17-4)   2, 4, 6, 8, 51, 49, 47, 45, ...

Each one corresponds to a rule and there is nothing in the information conveyed by the example (17-1) which indicates which of the three rules, or possibly a fourth rule, is actually used in the example. Therefore a learner cannot know which rule the teacher tries to teach him.

The example used by Kripke is the following. He considers two two-place functions *plus* and *quus*. They are recursive functions defined by

(17-5)   m plus n = m + n

and

(17-6)   m quus n = m + n   if $m, n \leq 57$
         m quus n = 5   if $m > 57$ or $n > 57$

where + in both definitions is determined by some standard addition algorithm. A person being taught addition by examples of addition of pairs of numbers which are all smaller than or equal to 57 cannot know whether the rule used and taught by the teacher is plus or quus (or possibly a third rule).

2.18 REMARK. Kripke's argument uses recursive functions. In (17-6), he uses definition of recursive functions by cases. It is therefore appropriate that we first define these concepts.

2.19 DEFINITION *(Recursive functions)*. The class of *recursive functions* is the smallest class of functions closed under the rules (RF1)-(RF4).
(RF1) *Basic functions: The zero functions*

$$Z_n: \underline{N}^n \to \underline{N} \qquad n \geq 0$$

(19-1) $Z_n(\mathbf{x}) = 0$

the successor function

$$S: \underline{N} \to \underline{N}$$

(19-2) $S(x) = x + 1$

the projection functions

$$U_{n,i}: \underline{N}^n \to \underline{N}$$

(19-3) $U_{n,i}(x_1, ..., x_i, ..., x_n) = x_i$ for $n > 0$ and $1 \leq i \leq n$

are recursive.

(RF2) *Substitution:* Let

$$g: \underline{N}^n \to \underline{N} \qquad \text{for } n > 0$$

$$h_i: \underline{N}^m \to \underline{N} \qquad \text{for } m \geq 0 \text{ and } 1 \leq i \leq n$$

be recursive. Then

$$f: \underline{N}^m \to \underline{N}$$

(19-4) $f(\mathbf{x}) = g(h_1(\mathbf{x}), ..., h_n(\mathbf{x}))$

is recursive where $\mathbf{x} = (x_1, ..., x_m)$.

(RF3) *Primitive recursion:* Let

$$g: \underline{N}^n \to \underline{N}$$
$$h: \underline{N}^{n+2} \to \underline{N}$$

be recursive. Then

$$f: \underline{N}^{n+1} \to \underline{N}$$

(19-5) $f(\mathbf{x}, 0) = g(\mathbf{x})$

$f(\mathbf{x}, y+1) = h(\mathbf{x}, y, f(\mathbf{x}, y))$

is recursive.

(RF4) *Minimisation:* Let $g: \underline{N}^{n+1} \to \underline{N}$ be recursive, and assume that

$$\forall \mathbf{x} \exists y \; g(\mathbf{x}, y) = 0$$

Then

$$f: \underline{N}^n \to \underline{N}$$

(19-6) $f(\mathbf{x}) = \mu y \, (g(\mathbf{x}, y) = 0)$

is recursive where $\mu y \, (...y...)$ denotes the smallest number $y \in \underline{N}$ which satisfies the condition $(...y...)$.

2.20 DEFINITION *(Characteristic function)*. Let $R \subseteq \underline{N}^n$ be an n-place relation (a set if n = 1).

(I) The *characteristic function* K_R of R is the function

$$K_R: \underline{N}^n \to \underline{N}$$

$$K_R(\mathbf{x}) = 1 \quad \text{if } \mathbf{x} \in R$$

$$K_R(\mathbf{x}) = 0 \quad \text{if } \mathbf{x} \notin R$$

(II) R is *recursive* iff K_R is recursive.

2.21 LEMMA *(Definition by cases)*. Let

$$f, g_1, ..., g_k: \underline{N}^n \to \underline{N}$$

$$R_1, ..., R_k \subseteq \underline{N}^n$$

such that for each $\mathbf{x}$ exactly one of $R_1(\mathbf{x}), ..., R_k(\mathbf{x})$ is true. Let f satisfy

(21-1) $\quad f(\mathbf{x}) = g_1(\mathbf{x}) \quad\quad\quad$ if $R_1(\mathbf{x})$

$\quad\quad\quad$ .... $\quad\quad\quad\quad\quad\quad\quad$ ....

$\quad\quad\quad f(\mathbf{x}) = g_k(\mathbf{x}) \quad\quad\quad$ if $R_k(\mathbf{x})$

If the g_i and R_j are all recursive, then f is recursive.

PROOF:

Since f has the explicit definition

(21-2) $\quad f(\mathbf{x}) = g_1(\mathbf{x}) \times K_{R_1}(\mathbf{x}) + ... + g_k(\mathbf{x}) \times K_{R_k}(\mathbf{x})$

and addition and multiplication are recursive, f is recursive.

2.22 REMARK *(continued)*. (I) When we inspect Definition 2.19, we see that all recursive functions, and hence all rules, can be defined completely for all values of the argument. We also see that no use of definition by cases is needed. Therefore the kind of problem which Kripke points to can always be circumvented. The basic functions in (RF1) are all explicitly defined for all values of the argument. Similarly, a function defined by substitution (RF2) is explicitly defined for all **x**. Finally (RF3) (primitive recursion) and (RF4) (minimisation) give procedures for systematically generating the value of f for all arguments. At first glance there seems to be a problem with the successor function. It might seem that we can learn this function only by examples: 1 is the successor of 0; 2 is the successor of 1, etc. The explanation is the following. Functions take numbers as input; but an algorithm takes only something concrete like numerals as input. To define the recursive functions, which are meant to be mathematical representations of numerical algorithms, we need a system of numerals, that is, a method of counting. One simple system is obtained by letting '0' represent null and obtain the other numerals by appending primes to '0':

$$0, 0', 0'', 0''', \ldots$$

Then the algorithm corresponding to the successor function is the following:

For a numeral n as input, return the same numeral with one more prime appended.

This is the algorithm for counting. The algorithm also defines completely the successor function S for all x.

(II) Though rules can always be defined without using the expedients of definition by finite sets of examples and definition by cases, these methods are often convenient in practice. How can they function in a teacher-learner relation? From identity (21-2), we see that a definition of a rule f by cases must contain adequate information about all the different cases. If f is defined by examples, the teacher is obliged to provide examples which adequately illustrate all the different cases $R_1(\mathbf{x}), \ldots, R_k(\mathbf{x})$. If the initial segment 2, 4, 6, 8 illustrate all the cases, it can only be an initial segment of the function $f(x) = 2(x+1)$. Any function with (17-3) or (17-4) as initial segment must be defined by a recursive procedure involving more than one case which are not all illustrated by 2, 4, 6, 8. Similarly, plus can be defined by only one case while quus needs at least two cases. In the case of quus, a definition by examples involving only numbers less than or equal to 57 does not contain adequate illustrations of all the cases. Therefore such examples alone can define only plus.

(III) Part (II) solves the Kripke problem when there is a teacher. Now consider the following situation. A person P visits a foreign country whose language he does not know. P tries to learn the language by observing how the native speakers use it. To do that, P must try to learn the semantic and grammatical rules of the language from examples. Even in this case, Kripke's objection is not valid. The reason is that definitions by cases are used in a special way in natural languages. An expression like f is assigned one meaning in situations which satisfy R_1 and another meaning in situations which satisfy R_2, etc. P must learn to distinguish between the situations $R_1, ..., R_k$ and identify the meanings attached to f in each type of situation. When P has learned the meaning of f in situations of type R_1, he can use f in such situations. This does not lead him to use f in the same way in situations of type R_2 because not all markers of situations of type R_1 are present in situations of type R_2. Illustrations which show that natural languages work like this can be found in any dictionary. When P has learned to attach the meaning $f(x) = g_1(x)$ to f in situations R_1, then he has learned partially how to use f. He can then later add to his knowledge of the language by learning the meaning of f, $f(x) = g_2(x)$, in situations of type R_2, etc. There are at least two advantages about organising a natural language according to this pattern. Expressions like f are in situations like R_1 associated with a natural pre-linguistic meaning which makes the association fairly easy to remember. Knowledge of the different uses of an expression, like f, can be learned step by step. This allows linguistic competence to grow organically. Moreover, a speaker rarely needs, and therefore rarely needs learn, the meaning of an expression in all cases of its use.

For grammatical rules, the situation is different. For instance, it is at least partly conventional how verbs are conjugated. In this case, the problem of finding the right conjugation for a verb is eased by the fact that generally, for any natural language, there are a few main rules for the conjugation of verbs plus a number of exceptions from these rules. It must be so since otherwise the grammar becomes too complicated to learn even for native speakers. A student of the language must proceed by identifying the few main rules and, step by step, the verbs which follow them and also the conjugation patterns of the exceptions to the main rules. For every step forward, he masters a larger portion of the language. The everything-or-nothing situation in Kripke's example with definition by cases does not arise in natural languages.

2.23 REMARK. The private language argument has, or ought to have, the following structure:

(23-1) By definition, a private language cannot be used for interpersonal communication. (Apparently Wittgenstein tries to show also that there is not and cannot be any private language; but he does not need this stronger conclusion for his purposes in philosophy of mind.)

(23-2) Since ordinary psychological language can be and is used successfully for interpersonal communication, it cannot be private.

(23-3) If psychological terms like "pain", "pleasure", and "sensation" had referred to something inner and private, they should belong to a private language.

(23-4) Therefore psychological terms do not refer to something inner and private.

There is some uncertainty about what Wittgenstein meant by the private language argument. In particular, what did he mean by "an inner and private state?" There are two reasonable interpretations: (1) A state in a person P is inner and private if and only if it belongs to the immaterial soul of P, in the sense of a Cartesian psycho-physical dualism. (2) A state in P is inner and private if and only if it is a state in P's central nervous system which is directly accessible to P himself via his self-awareness.

One interpretation of the private language argument could be that Wittgenstein only wanted to refute the existence of states of type (1) by showing that if states of type (1) existed, reference to an inner state would make the language private. This weaker interpretation should make some of the statements and examples adduced by Wittgenstein in the private language argument meaningful and correct. The interpretation of the private language argument actually used in Section 1 above is somewhat stronger, namely that Wittgenstein wanted to show the validity of Thesis (10-1) in § 1.10 which excludes reference to inner states in both of the senses (1) and (2) defined above. Some of the formulations in the paragraphs on the private language argument in *Philosophische Untersuchungen* support this interpretation. Even if his intention was to consider only inner, private states in the first sense, the interpretation he himself actually gives of the private language argument is that he has excluded reference to inner, private states in both of the senses (1) and (2). This can be seen from the fact that some of the consequences that he draws from the argument are valid only if he includes both senses of "inner and private state" in the argument. In particular, if Wittgenstein had been concerned only with states in the sense (1), he should not have been forced to identify meaning with use in the language in the way shown in the analysis in Remark 2.2 of the present section but should at least have discussed the alternative of identifying meaning with something in a speaker's mind, that is, something in the brain and accessible by introspection. It appears that Wittgenstein failed, in the present context, to distinguish between the two senses (1) and (2) above of "inner and private state". Because the private language argument is the fundamental building block in Wittgenstein's later philosophy, for instance in the theory of meaning and in the therapeutic conception of philosophy, this failure turns out to be disastrous for his endeavours.

Wittgenstein is concerned with philosophy of mind in the private language argument. The philosophy of mind defended in the present essay is the following. A normal human being has a brain. States, processes, and events in the brain can be studied from the outside (by for instance neurological and psychological methods and observation of behaviour); but they can also be studied from the inside. Via the self-awareness, the brain can observe some of its own states, processes, and events from the inside. Thus the mind satisfies the following condition.

(23-5) *A person P's mind = P's direct consciousness (both as act and content) of states, processes, and events in P's own brain.*

This is mainly the Cartesian conception, though without any ontological psycho-physical dualism. The analysis in Section 1 shows that the private language argument does not exclude this kind of philosophy of mind, and it shows that the private language argument does not exclude reference to inner and private states, processes and events in the sense (2).

UNGROUNDED SEMANTICS:
SEARLE'S CHINESE ROOM THOUGHT EXPERIMENT, THE FAILURE OF META- AND SUBSYSTEMIC UNDERSTANDING, AND SOME THOUGHTS ABOUT THOUGHT-EXPERIMENTS

CHRISTIAN BEENFELDT

University College, Oxford
The Danish National Research Foundation: Center for Subjectivity Research
University of Copenhagen

1. Syntax and Semantics in the Chinese Room Argument

With the 2002 anthology *Views Into the Chinese Room* published by Oxford University Press, John Searle's famous Chinese Room Argument was subject to yet another round of debate – some 22 years since its original introduction in an 1980 issue of the *Behavioral and Brain Sciences*.[1] From its very first appearance the argument clearly touched a nerve – as evidenced by the 27 peer-review commentaries that Searle's paper immediately elicited – and in subsequent years, hundreds of articles discussing the argument have been written by philosophers, psychologists, cognitive scientists and Artificial Intelligence researchers alike, with evaluations of the argument spanning the entire spectrum from the very critical to the highly laudatory.[2] Preston goes as far as to characterize the argument as "contemporary philosophy's best-known argument"[3] and Dietrich states that "AI would have no future if Searle is correct."[4] Although both are overselling the point here, there *is* widespread agreement about the substantial importance of Searle's argument to the issue of machine thinking. As Teng puts it:

> Searle's... Chinese room argument has been one of the most celebrated philosophical arguments in the contemporary philosophy of mind. It is simple and elegant, and is the best-known and most-cited philosophical argument against Strong AI.[5][6]

Searle's argument runs as follows. Imagine yourself locked in a room with several baskets full of Chinese symbols and assume that you do not understand a word of Chinese. You are given a rulebook in English for manipulating Chinese symbols *strictly* in terms of their formal characteristics and intersymbolic interrelationship, not their meaning. Now some Chinese symbols are passed into the room and you are instructed to send Chinese symbols out of the room, all in accordance with the rulebook specifications, where a rule might say, for example, "Take a squiggle-squiggle sign out of the basket number one and put it next to a squoggle-squoggle sign from basket number two."[7] What really goes on, you later learn, is that a group of computer programmers have written a program to simulate the understanding of Chinese, enabling the entity executing it to answer questions in that language by matching the input against its memory and producing a suitable prefabricated Chinese response as the output. Unbeknown to you, people outside the room refer to the symbols send into the room as "questions" and the symbols you pass back out of the room as "answers to questions" and since the rules are so well written, the symbols so well arranged, and your symbol manipulations conducted with such a degree of expeditious adroitness, the room as a whole achieves indistinguishability with a native speaker of Chinese.[8] If this is all the case, you – plus the room, the rules and the baskets of symbols – will in principle be able to pass the Turing Test,[9] and the room (with all its viscera, including you) will accordingly be regarded as an intelligent speaker of Chinese. Yet, the point the story is that while to external observers it seems as if there is someone in the room who understands Chinese, you have no such understanding – and, worse still, there is apparently no way for you ever to learn Chinese by the method of simply manipulating such formal symbols.[10] If, accordingly, you can complete a sequence of discretely specified symbol manipulation routines while being utterly incognizant of their meaning, and thus can pass a Turing Test, then so can a digital computer; it is, indeed, the very ability to perform calculating operations on *any* purely formal computational content that is the very source of power for such a device.

To carve the point about the absence of meaning inside the Chinese Room into high relief, contrast the process of manipulating uninterpretable symbols according to strictly formal characteristics, with the process of answering questions in English, where one is cognizant not only of the formal characteristics of the symbols but also of their meaning. For example, compare replying 000100101011 to the question 00111101101010001, with answering, say, "toast" to the question "what did you eat for breakfast?" The intuitive thrust of the Chinese Room Argument thus derives from the fact that the Chinese symbols appear to the symbol manipulator as mere *syntax*, consisting exclusively of formal characteristics and patterns of formation, while English symbols also afford him some understanding of the relevant *semantics*. The general syntax-semantics distinction is one that goes back at least as far as the 1938 publication of Charles Morris' *Foundations of the Theory of Signs*,[11] in which the latter argues that *semiosis*, the process in which something functions as a sign, consists of the following three central elements:

1. Syntactics, the study of the pure relation of signs to other signs, in abstraction from the relations of signs to objects or to interpreters.[12]
2. Semantics, the study of the relation of signs to their designata, to the objects that the sign denotes.[13]
3. Pragmatics, the study of the relation of signs to their users.[14]

In relation to Searle's argument, the point is that one can and must distinguish between *sign vehicles* and *designata* – i.e. between the formal characteristics of symbols (syntactics) on the one hand, and the issue of what the symbols are symbols of (semantics) on the other. The problem for the Chinese Room inhabitant, therefore, lies in his inability to reach the semantics of the symbols he manipulates, manifesting what Harnad calls the *Symbol Grounding Problem* – i.e. the problem of connecting symbols to what they are about without the mediation of external interpretation.[15] Human beings, accordingly, are not limited to an exchange of uninterpreted syntax, because we interact with the world of "objects, events and states" and thereby afford the grounding of our symbols. As an example, take the pomiferous fruit found on certain deciduous trees of the rose family known in English as an "apple". Having seen, manipulated and eaten such fruits, and having learned that the semiotic unit "apple" refers to them, the symbol has been thoroughly grounded for a normal English speaker – and in subsequent encounters with the symbol "apple" he consequently has not merely syntax, but syntax plus semantics. To an ungrounded *symbol system*[16] like the Chinese Room, by contrast, the meaning of the symbols manipulated cannot arise endogenously within the structure of uninterpreted symbols and shape-based rules for their manipulation, the shape of which is essentially arbitrary in relation to what the symbols are interpretable as meaning. The symbols used by the symbol manipulator are, rather, ungrounded in the sense that they can only refer to, and be defined in terms of, other equally unintelligible symbols – and so the person in the room is chained to an eternally free-floating merry-go-round of uninterpretable Chinese syntax. To look for meaning within such a system is analogous to the pursuance of meaning in a Chinese to Chinese dictionary when one is ignorant of Chinese in the first place: everything may be contained in the dictionary (definitions, examples of usage, etymology etc.) but one is unable to get beyond the syntactical level to the actual content. Looking up one definition of a word will only take one to another, i.e. to more uninterpretable syntax, and however much one inspects the symbols contained in the dictionary, one will never get to their *meaning* without the requisite grounding; all one procures is one more gyration on the syntactical merry-go-round. While locked inside the room there is no possibility of stepping outside the ungrounded syntactical system and – pointing to our pomiferous fruit – affirming that "by 'apple' I mean *this*". Cognition, accordingly, cannot be just symbol manipulation, as it must also involve the grounding of the symbols, i.e. the connection of the syntax with the semantics, ultimately rooted in sensory experience and direct interaction with the environment. The whole symbol system, of course, is systematically interpretable as meaningful, provided there is an external interpreter for whom the symbols are already grounded and who facilitates the mediation of the interpretation. The problem is that there appears to be no way to achieve the perspective of a grounded external interpreter for someone locked inside the Chinese Room – and if there is no grounded interpretation, there is no *understanding*, and therefore there cannot reasonably be said to be the human-level mentality ascribed by the Turing Test[17] to the subject in question. As the result of all this, the classical functional conception of mentality, Turing mechanism, machine functionalism and the multiple realizability of mental states assumption all appear to be equally impugned by the Chinese Room scenario. In a terse statement of its logical structure, Searle sums up the structure of the Chinese Room Argument as follows:

1. Programs are formal (syntactical).
2. Minds have content (semantics).
3. Syntax is not sufficient for semantics.

From which the conclusion follows that programs are not minds.[18]

Searle holds that computers might have minds for other reasons, but the point here is that the program alone will not guarantee mentality.

Let us now turn to some of the major replies that have been made to Searle's argument, including arguments recently put forth by Block, Haugeland and others.

2. Metasystemic Understanding?

First consider the *System Reply,* by far the most prominent reply to Searle's argument and one that has "from the earliest outings" been the "standard reply from people in AI", as Dennett has observed.[19] According to Turing biographer Andrew Hodges, it furthermore seems that Turing himself would have agreed with it.[20] To specify the exact claim of this reply, let us note that Searle's Gedankenexperiment can be formulated as the following argument against the Turing Test:

1. The Chinese Room can exhibit relevant functional isomorphism with a competent speaker of Chinese within the Turing Test domain of investigation.
2. The Chinese Room has no understanding.
3. Understanding can reasonably be said to be a precondition of human-like intelligence.

Ergo, the Turing Test is unreliable in its ascription of intelligence.

Opposing premise (2), the System Reply is the claim that there really *is* understanding somewhere in the Chinese Room "system" – the "system" consisting of Searle + room + databank + bits of paper. The person in the room may not understand Chinese, but the entire system, in other words, does. As Copeland argues:

> Told fairly, the tale [i.e. the Chinese Room Argument] contains two principal characters – Joe Soap, the tireless labourer, and the System, whose exotic conversation emanates from the Output slot... [Joe] is, after all nothing more than a cog in the machinery. What we want to know is whether the *System* understands.[21]

We saw earlier that the assumed lack of understanding of the room hinges on the introspective report of the symbol manipulator. It hinges, in other words, on you, the reader, imaginatively placing yourself in the position of the symbol manipulator and recognizing his lack understanding. Yet, according to the System Reply, the symbol manipulator is only one cogwheel in a great machine – a cogwheel that is unable to apprehend the whole of which it is merely one composant. Put in terms of a digital computer, the symbol-manipulating homunculus is merely the Central Processing Unit (CPU), the main operating part of the machine that carries out operation according to the instructions provided by the software. An operational digital computer, however, also consists of software, an input device, an output device and a storage device and, as a whole, these components can execute a program (a game of computer chess, say) which no component alone can do. Accordingly, if one were to adopt the isolated perspective of the CPU alone, one would conclude that the digital computer is merely crunching meaningless strings of binary digits. On the level of the whole system, however, it is apparent that the digital computer *is* executing a game of chess.

Although this reply might appear to have some initial plausibility, a major defect of it is that it ignores the fact that the Chinese Room inhabitant is the only component of the system which, when it comes to understanding, is in that *line of business*. To see this, consider the following analogy. John, a lazy college freshman, is to take a written exam in ancient philosophy – a subject he never bothered to study at all. Keen to have him pass, his ardent classical functionalist father devices the following system: John is to match the questions (e.g. "What was the role give by Heraclitus to Fire?") with an appropriate answer found by looking up the appropriate symbol strings (e.g. "Heraclitus" and "Fire") on corresponding pieces of paper, according to an ingenious scheme that will guarantee examination success. John has no understanding of the names or terms involved – to him "Heraclitus" sounds like a particularly painful skin infection – but he agrees to have all these notes hidden in various places on his person, allowing him to surreptitiously copy down the (to him) unintelligible answers at the exam. Let's say that he is not caught using this system and consequently acquires remarkably good grades in ancient philosophy. Eventually, however, he has a moral change of heart and confesses the true state of affairs to his teacher. The following conversation between the father and the professor might thus ensue.

Professor: John was cheating and has no understanding of ancient philosophy whatever. I am going to give him an F on the exam.
Father: What on earth do you mean? His answers were functionally isomorphic with those of a diligent student, weren't they?
Professor: Yes. But he merely gave the same answer at the exam that a diligent student would have, while, in fact, having no understanding of ancient philosophy whatever.
Father: How do you know?
Professor: Let's ask John.

Father: That won't tell you anything. John might not understand ancient philosophy, but the *John Exam Taking System* – John + the scheme for using the hidden notes + the notes + the examination questions – obviously does understand ancient philosophy. How else could John have acquired such good grades? So, go ahead and take a few points off John's grade for smuggling hidden notes, but don't claim that the system present at the exam didn't understand ancient philosophy!

Clearly, the father is making a patently absurd claim – that cheating at an exam and not being caught at it, amounts to having a genuine understanding of the subject matter. *Hidden notes and schemes are not in the business of understanding*, and if John doesn't understand, then neither does the system. The system might appear to understand – it might be functionally isomorphic within a limited domain of investigation with a student that *does* understand ancient philosophy, but that plainly is a different matter.

Another way to show that the central claim of the System Reply is specious – i.e. another way to show that it is plainly wrong to maintain that the room, the databank and the bits of paper in some mysterious way combine with the person in the room to create a supersystem, on the analogy of the computer system – is simply to remove those elements from the scenario and still produce the same effect. Searle does this with a very simple maneuver known as *the internalization move*. The idea with that move is that all the elements of the system are to be internalized in the symbol manipulator – who has no understanding of Chinese, as he himself can attest to – thus removing anything that could be regarded as a system above, beyond or around him. The "man + program + board + paper + input and output doors" system has then been eliminated. To put this in terms of the Chinese Room Argument scenario, the imagined person inside the Chinese room has now memorized the instruction book using his photographic memory and, to get rid of the room itself, we might even suppose that he works outdoors. Now there really is *nothing* in the supposed "system" that is not at the same time simply in the man – in other words, the symbol manipulator in the new outdoor Chinese "Room" has become the system, providing us with a full report from the level of the whole aggregate and not merely from the limited perspective of a cogwheel inside a complicated machine. And it is a report plainly revealing that the he understands as little after the move as he did when he was inside the Chinese Room shuffling symbols. During the new outdoor Turing Test, for example, he has memorized that sound pattern 21,428 activates response category 529,329, that sound pattern 934 activates response category 112,332 and that sound pattern 98,937 activates response category 8,121, and that if response category 529,329, 112,332 and 8,121 are activated in that order during state 147, his response must be sound pattern 902,482. From this, he still has no means of grasping the meaning of the question, e.g. "which novel is your favorite?" – nor of his answer to the question, e.g. "*Les Misérables*". He might actually have liked Hugo's *Toilers of the Sea* or *The Man Who Laughed* better, or never had time to read any of them (being too busy memorizing meaningless strings of symbols, no doubt), but none of this will ever come up since he is wholly ignorant of the meaning of the sounds he is hearing and uttering. While the amount of memorization required for outdoor symbol manipulator to perform internalized syntactical manipulations of this magnitude and complexity is of indisputable counterfactual proportions, it seems no more counterfactual than the supposition that the person in the room could imitate a Chinese speaker by physically manipulating symbols.

3. Houser's English Tourist

One attempt to counter the internalization move has been made by Hauser, employing what we can call the *English Tourist Reply*.[22] With that, Hauser aims to examine more closely the process by which the Chinese Room inhabitant performs the syntax memorization required to exhibit functional isomorphism with a Chinese speaker. As an analogy to the Chinese Room, we are invited to imagine an English tourist attempting to speak Chinese. At first, while the tourist depends entirely upon his Chinese phrase book, we would not credit him with any understanding of Chinese. At this point, he is like the person in the room *before* the internalization move, merely shuffling incomprehensible syntactical symbols. After the material has been memorized, however, we see the tourist able to converse fluently with native Chinese speakers without relying upon the phrase book any more. This is apparently like the symbol manipulator after the internalization move. To such a tourist we would characteristically not be so quick in denying an understanding of Chinese, even if he voices an introspectively based disavowal of understanding – a disavowal, by the way, that he would only maintain in English and not, ex hypothesi, in Chinese, since that would instantly disrobe him during a standard Turing Test.

> Suppose we take seriously the idea the Searle-in-the-room is passing Turing's Test in Chinese – conversing (or corresponding) with native Chinese speakers, in real time, with such fluency that these other Chinese speakers could conclude he understands... Now we are asked to imagine that Searle ... memorizes the rules and symbols and fluently converses (or corresponds) with his Chinese Interlocutors by consciously applying the memorized rules. I, for one, am by no means confident that I can say *what* private experiences or subjective impressions of understanding would or wouldn't accompany such a remarkable performance.[23]

The problem with Hauser's reply is that the example of the English tourist is relevantly disanalogous to the state of affairs in the Chinese Room. In fact, Hauser has changed the fundamental premises of the thought experiment, and is basing his argument on a substantially dissimilar scenario. The person in the Chinese Room merely manipulates syntax and so does the person outside the room with the rules and databank memorized. It that what an English tourist does? Well, no. A tourist is actually engaged in the rudimentary learning of semantics, not merely the manipulation of ungrounded syntax. A phrase book does not consist of entries on this order: "whenever you hear 'asdjk sdf jkf' reply with 'ffesr rwer slasd' and do not worry about the meaning of this exchange". Rather, a phrase book will tell you "'asdjk sdf jkf' means 'it is nice weather today'" and "'ffesr rwer slasd' means 'yes, it's wonderfully sunny'". Using a phrase book, like learning a second language, is thus parasitic upon the semantics one has already acquired via one's native language. One merely acquires the subsequent understanding that a different set of syntactic symbols "asdjk sdf jkf" rather than "it is nice weather today" performs the same semantic function. To posit the semiotical equivalence of the English tourist and the Chinese Room inhabitant, as Hauser does, is to commit what may be termed the fallacy of the surreptitiously introduced parasitic symbol grounding. This fallacy consists in treating as strongly analogous two systems of which one (the Chinese Room inhabitant) is a closed and ungrounded syntactical system, and the other (the English tourist) is a unclosed and grounded system, and in that process relying upon the indirect and parasitic use of pre-existing semantics (English words and their meaning in the native vocabulary of the tourist).

Besides the parasitic symbol grounding afforded by the phrase book, of course, the English tourist would also have a direct means of acquiring the symbol grounding of Chinese syntax, namely via the deployment of words and phrases accompanied by pointing to actual things (a cup, a bird, a tree, a car etc.), affording an understanding of Chinese by the observation of non-verbal responses exhibited by competent Chinese speakers. In order to eliminate this direct symbol grounding, we need simply assume that the English tourist is memorizing his phrase book in a community of exclusively English-speaking language users, and that he learns to speak Chinese without ever going to China. In order to eliminate indirect symbol grounding and thereby also immunize ourselves from the fallacy of surreptitiously introduced parasitic symbol grounding, we need merely consider the plight of a Chinese to Japanese phrase-book memorizer – i.e. the plight of an exclusively English-speaking tourist trying to learn Chinese from a Chinese-Japanese phrase book alone. Such a speaker, like the Chinese Room inhabitant, has no way of forming a connection between his English semantics and the syntax he manipulates. In this reformulation of the scenario, the fallacy of the surreptitiously introduced parasitic symbol grounding is effectively avoided and we see that even if the phrase book memorizer were to memorize the entire Chinese to Japanese phrase book perfectly, it would provide him with no understanding – no semantics – of either language. He would be riding the syntactical merry-go-round, passing from ungrounded Chinese symbols to ungrounded Japanese symbols, with no access to the grounding of either. On the other hand, once symbol grounding is introduced to one of the symbol sets, i.e. once the tourist comes to understand either Chinese or Japanese – by directly grounding it with the help of Chinese or Japanese speakers or by grounding it indirectly via a parasitical connection to his English semantics – an understanding of the other set would in principle follow readily.

4. Subsystemic Understanding?

Another move has then been suggested by Block,[24] Haugeland,[25] McDermott,[26] and others, according to which the basic System Reply is, in effect, relocated to the subsystemic level. We can call this argument the *Subsystem Reply*, and characterize it as the contention that there is an understanding of Chinese at a subsystemic level in the Chinese Room setup – before and/or after the internalization move has been made. McDermott:

> ... there are *two* "persons" in the [Chinese] room (or there would be with a few changes to the setup). They happen to share the same hardware, and so our commensense ideas about counting persons gets confused, but there they are.[27]

Block:

> 'But how can it be', Searle would object, 'that you implement a system that understands Chinese even though *you* don't understand Chinese?' The Systems Reply rejoinder is that you implement a Chinese understanding system without yourself understanding Chinese or necessarily even being aware of what you are doing under that description.[28]

The original System Reply was aptly expressed by Block's statement that the "man + program + board + paper + input and output doors" constituted a system capable of understanding – above and beyond the reported lack of understanding maintained by the symbol manipulator. The Subsystem Reply, by contrast, contends that the system capable of understanding is not *above and beyond* the symbol manipulator – but rather – *below and subliminal* to him. So, while the System Reply was vanquished by the internalization move which brought the entire metasystemic level into introspective awareness of the Chinese Room inhabitant, the Subsystem Reply appears to be unharmed by that strategy since the proposed subsystemic understanding still remains inaccessible to the symbol manipulator after all the elements of the system have been internalized. To frame this reply in terms of the Turing Test, we can say that when the symbol manipulator performs his syntactical routines, a Chinese understanding system arises within him that, unbeknown to him, understands the conversation that is taking place. The adequacy of the Turing Test consequently appears not to be not overturned by the Chinese Room counterexample: there *is*, in other words, a genuinely intelligent being that understands the conversation to be found in the Turing Test-passing Chinese Room, a being that just happens to reside at a lower systemic level than Searle had erroneously supposed.

If we look closely at the System Reply, we can differentiate two different, if closely related, variants of the view. The first variant, exemplified by McDermott's position, maintains that there is Chinese understanding at the subsystemic level in the symbol manipulator *before* the internalization move is made. Let us call this the *Pre-Internalization Move System Reply*. The second variant, exemplified by Block's position, maintains that there is Chinese understanding in the symbol manipulator *after* the internalization move is made. We can call this the *Post-Internalization Move System Reply*.

Let us first examine the Pre-Internalization Move System Reply. Here, McDermott contends that there are four systems and two "persons" inside the room:

1. The person's brain that keeps the body alive and well.
2. Manfred, the person who introspects and speaks English.
3. The person as a computer, given the role the person has chosen to play (i.e. given that he has agreed to shuffle symbols during a Turing Test).
4. Wong, the person who understands Chinese.[29]

Wong is the only "person" that can safeguard the validity of the Turing Test in the face of Searle's argument, since he is the only being in the room assumed to understand Chinese – so what is McDermott's argument for his emergence? Well, here's the story: Suppose that Manfred, manipulating meaningless syntax all day wants to keep track of some occasional squiggles (McDermott calls this "memories"), and does so in a notebook "which he adds to and refers to over the days". He will write in Chinese such things as "Wong just had a sensation of moo shi pork...", "Wong decided, after much soul searching, that x was better than y", and "Wong wishes you would find someone smarter than this turkey Manfred to implement him".[30] Assume Manfred is eventually fired and Humbert is put in his place. Humbert will also (for the same undisclosed reason), take up Manfred's notebook-writing habit, and will write things as "Wong is pleased, for Humbert performs much faster than Manfred did."[31] Wong, it may be said, is the multiple personality disorder of the Chinese Room. Since Wong is conscious, understands Chinese, holds beliefs and has preferences apparently of his own volition, there seems to be no sound basis on which to deny him the status of an intelligent being.

In the Post-Internalization Move System Reply, someone similar to Wong can be said to exist as part of the symbol manipulator. In making the case for this, Block invites us to imagine that – granting Searle's internalization move – the symbol manipulator has fully internalized the data bank and all the other Chinese Room appurtenances, and is doing the symbol manipulations in his head on a nine-to-five basis. Continuing from the first-person perspective, you – the symbol manipulator – will respond to all English utterances during working-hours with "a request in Chinese to speak Chinese", being so intent on performing the task of mental syntax manipulation and perhaps also being somewhat obsessive about it. At 5 p.m. you stop working and become a regular monolingual English speaker. Why do we then say that you implement a Chinese system, rather than that a Chinese system implements you? Block:

>Because you (the English system whom I am now addressing) are following the instructions of a program in English to make Chinese noises and not the other way around.[32]

Block concludes, however, that although you may have the upper hand in the asymmetrical relationship, since he depends for his existence upon your actions in a way that you do not depend upon his, your body is nevertheless subject to a thinking cohabitant. He makes two major points in support of this conclusion:

1. The Chinese system has "plans" and makes "decisions" – he could, for example, decide to "become a magician."[33]
2. The person doing the manipulations may well be unaware of his other self, but this is irrelevant since "real cases of multiple personalities are often cases in which one personality is unaware of the others."[34]

Point (1), in other words, reaffirms the status of the subsystemic being as an intelligent person, while point (2) reaffirms the appeal to the McDermottesque idea of multiple personality disorder in the Chinese Room scenario. Returning to the common denominator between McDermott's and Block's respective versions of the System Reply, we see that both maintain the existence of a genuine intelligent consciousness that understands Chinese inside the symbol manipulator, thereby justifying the Turing Test in its ascription of intelligence to the Chinese Room system.

The Subsystem Reply, however, does not appear to be successful. In general terms, it repeats the error of the Hauser's English Tourist Reply, ascribing an understanding of Chinese semantics to the subsystemic consciousness inside the room that is absolutely unobtainable from within the confines of an entirely ungrounded syntactical system. The question is *how* anyone tied to an ungrounded syntactical merry-go-round could acquire an understanding of the semantics of the symbols he manipulates, enabling him to express his views and preferences. The Searlean answer, of course, is that this is altogether impossible, and that no such view could be expressed in Chinese inside the room since this would presuppose an access to Chinese semantics that is exclusively available *outside* the room. The contraposed functionalist position is that there must somehow be understanding inside the room, since the Chinese Room is functionally isomorphic with a competent Chinese speaker, so he – or some part of him – must necessarily understand Chinese. We have returned, in other words, to a point in the dialectic that closely mirrors a point we reached when considering the System Reply. In the latter case, we saw that the same effect could be produced without all the extraneous elements that were claimed to somehow combine with the symbol manipulator to create a larger "system". Is there some conceptual move that can similarly break this impasse, revealing – like the internalization move did at the metasystemic level – that there really is no understanding on the subsystemic level either? Sure. We can call this the *Chinese Mansion* and the *Chinese Memorizer Queue Move*, depending on whether it is executed apart from, or in conjunction with the internalization move – i.e. depending on whether it is directed against the Pre-Internalization Move System Reply or the Post-Internalization Move System Reply.

Let us begin with the reply to the Pre-Internalization Move System Reply. Accordingly, imagine that, to decisively resolve the System Reply-Chinese Room dispute, a philosophically minded contractor is hired to add a few modifications to the Chinese Room in preparation for the next Turing Test. On the two opposite sides of the symbol manipulator's room where the slots for in- and output are respectively located, the contractor attaches a vestibule. In each vestibule, a new symbol manipulator is placed, independently doing his syntactical routines unaware of the presence of the other symbol manipulators. The vestibule to the left of the main room now receives the Chinese symbols and the vestibule to the right of the room delivers the replies. After this architectural enlargement, the building passes a Turing Test, and is ascribed intelligence accordingly. Let us call this new structure the *Chinese Mansion*. According to the Pre-Internalization Move System Reply the ascription of intelligence by the Turing Test is warranted by the presence of a subsystemic intelligence – some relative of Wong, perhaps – residing like a multiple personality inside the symbol manipulator in the Chinese Room. Keeping that in mind, let us take a closer look at the viscerous mechanics of the Chinese Mansion. What actually takes place is that the symbol manipulator in the left vestibule receives the Chinese symbols representing (unbeknown to him) the questions posed, matches them with unintelligible symbols according to principles of ironclad encryption, and sends the new symbols into the main room. The original Chinese Room symbol manipulator, unaware of the origin of the new and equally unintelligible symbols, matches them with other symbols according to the procedures of his rulebook, and sends out the latter through the slot to the right. Receiving his input, the symbol manipulator in the right vestibule matches it with Chinese symbols – unbeknown to him performing a decryption of the material – and sends out answers to the questions in flawless Chinese. Since the subsystemic consciousness is supposed to reside within the symbol manipulator, where are we to find that consciousness now? Certainly the inhabitant in the left vestibule, who merely performs the mechanical encryption of Chinese syntax and never accesses the mansion's replies to the questions posed, cannot house it. Nor can the original Chinese Room inhabitant, who merely matches encrypted symbols to encrypted symbols. Nor, finally, can the inhabitant in the right vestibule, who merely performs the mechanical decryptions of encrypted symbols to Chinese syntax with no access to the input. The point is that even if all three symbols manipulators were, incredibly, subject to a subsystemic inhabitant like Wong – and even if he miraculously came into existence with a perfect command of Chinese – no consciousness (normal or subsystemic) inside the Chinese Mansion is capable of understanding the verbal exchange that is taking place. In neither the main room nor the vestibules, in other words, is there an entire conversation to be understood, even by a fully competent speaker of Chinese. Thus, the postulation of a subsymbolic consciousness housed by one of the symbol manipulator will not protect the Turing Test's ascription of intelligence from the Chinese Room Argument – as exemplified by this minor reformulation of the argument that closes the door, as it were, on the subsystem vignette offered by McDermott, Block and others.

But what if, one might object, the central Chinese Room inhabitant was *somehow* able to break the encryption and get to the Chinese syntax? Then there would be a full conversation to be found in his room, wouldn't there? And that, in turn, would provide the basis for Wong's understanding of Chinese, wouldn't it? No. First of all, the Chinese Room inhabitant has no particular means of performing code breaking at his disposal – he has no books on the subject, no secret intelligence data to aid him, and no intercepted pieces of the code key to help him break the encryption.[35] Second, if one set of ironclad encryption is not enough to ensure the inaccessibility of the Chinese syntax inside the original Chinese Room, we can simply have the contractor add as many additional vestibules on either side of the room as is required – such that each vestibule on the left side performs the encryption to which only the corresponding vestibule on the right side has the decryption key. Thus, the Chinese Room inhabitant would be faced with not merely ironclad encrypted Chinese syntax, but with Chinese syntax encrypted in an ironclad manner 10, 100 or n-times over. Third, the Chinese Room inhabitant is *not even aware* that the syntax has been encrypted in the first place. One day, before the vestibules were added, he was manipulating unencrypted unintelligible symbols. The next day, after a sleepless night while the construction workers turned his lonely room into a sprawling mansion, he is still doing what he has always done – manipulate unintelligible symbols. Now, of course, the adherent of the Subsystem Reply may fall back to the position of the System Reply: You have effectively removed subsystemic understanding from the room, he might concede, but this only brings the understanding back to the metasystemic level of the arrangement. Accordingly, it is no longer the Chinese Room as a whole that should be said to understand, rather, it is the Chinese Mansion as a whole – symbol manipulators, main room, vestibules, encryption, decryption and all – that should be said to grasp the conversation that is taking place.

This brings me to the next thought-experiment – the *Chinese Memorizer Queue Move*. This move is simply the combination of Chinese Mansion and the internalization move. Thus, if the internalization move applied to the original Chinese Room arrangement produced one person standing outdoors doing symbol manipulations from memory – the same move applied to the Chinese Mansion produces a queue of symbol manipulators (three at least) whispering to each other outside, and respectively: (1) receiving Chinese syntax and encrypting it from memory, (2) manipulating encrypted data to produce other encrypted data according to memorized rules and, finally, (3) decrypting data to Chinese syntax from memory. Again in this case, the symbol memorizers have no means of breaking the encryption since the length of the queue may be increased illimitably to ensure truly ironclad encryption. Also, the original symbol manipulator in the middle of the queue is still unaware that he is receiving encrypted data, since – for all he knows – the sound symbols being exchanged are completely arbitrary, with no hidden semantics encrypted deep within them. Besides, he is used to strangers presenting him with unintelligible syntax to which he make equally unintelligible replies, and we can even assume that the symbol manipulation takes place in pitch darkness, so that he only sees the two symbol manipulators to his immediate left and right. As in the Chinese Mansion, the subsystemic consciousness postulated by Block to exist in the symbol memorizer has no means of understanding the conversation the Chinese Memorizer Queue as a whole is taking part in, even if that consciousness was to arise miraculously with a perfect understanding of Chinese. And, of course, he has no means of acquiring such an understanding in the

Chinese Memorizer Queue, since no member of that queue is ever exposed to a complete conversation in Chinese, each performing only encryption, decryption or the manipulation of encrypted data.

This, then, seems to close off the possibility of a Chinese-understanding consciousness on all the three systemic levels of the room that have been posited. On the ground level of the room, we know from the outset that there is no understanding of Chinese, since we imagine ourselves in the position of the symbol manipulator, attesting to our ignorance of Chinese under such circumstances. On the metasystemic level, we saw that there could be no understanding of Chinese as we brought the entire system into introspective awareness via the internalization move. On the subsystemic level, finally, we excluded the possibility of a Chinese-understanding system by making the entire conversation inaccessible to any individual symbol manipulator, and thus also to any subsystemic consciousness postulated to be housed by such individuals. Wherever we turn our gaze – to the level at hand, above or below us – we find no plausible basis for asserting that there is someone who understands Chinese.

5. The Epistemic Force of Thought Experiments

Having now, in other words, defended the Chinese Room Argument against various objections, I do want to end on a note of caution. Searle's imagined Chinese Room scenario is a *thought experiment*, as are the various more or less fantastic subsequent modifications to it that have appeared in the last 20-odd years. A typical thought experiment, in brief, is an imagined counterfactual scenario that is held to illuminate some real fact – and the obvious problem with this is that such arguments posit, and draw conclusions from, situations that realistically speaking are altogether *metaphysically impossible*. This should make us think seriously, and critically, about the epistemic force of such arguments.

The issue of the viability of a general deflationist stance towards thought experiments is both timely and interesting – but at present, I will have to limit myself to a much narrower issue, namely to a specific reply to the Chinese Room Argument that derives from certain less generalized considerations pertaining to the particular counterfactuality of the scenario itself. The person in the room could never, the reply might go, by the Chinese Room mechanics of symbol matching, produce answers quickly enough to actually imitate a native

Chinese speaker – he would have to rifle through millions of pages of script, and would require minutes, if not hours or days, to answer a simple question like "what is your favorite color". As Leiber puts it

> John Searle offers a[n]... argument in which he is to be imagined simulating an intelligent Chinese speaker by reading and sorting for him meaningless Chinese symbols; by any construal of his supposed counterexample, it would take Searle hours to respond to simple questions.[36]

The basic observation underpinning this complaint, of course, is undeniably true. The person in the room could not in fact work fast enough to actually satisfy the Turing Test.[37] The question is whether this is relevant. On the one hand, the Chinese Room Argument was never offered as a *practical* refutation of the Turing Test; it was, rather, offered as a means of illuminating a *theoretical* deficiency inherent in the functionalistic conception of the mind and the Turing Test's ascription of mentality. But does this, on the other hand, mean that thought experiments simply are disordinate epistemological free-for-alls, where any fanciful scenario may be afforded some nonnegligible measure of epistemic force and adduced as 'evidence' for some desired conclusion? Clearly not. If there is a value in thought experiments, it must lie in their very ability to single out and illuminate some genuine factor, by making practically impossible alterations to, or exaggerations of, certain other factors that are demonstrably irrelevant to the point at issue.

If one, therefore, grants some measure of epistemic force to thought experiments in general, it seems that Searle's argument fares quite well – in as much as the practically impossible exaggerations assumed by the argument are not ones that appear to be arbitrarily selected, but rather are ones that we have a strong prior justification from analogy for assuming to be reasonable. The Chinese Room, as we know, serves as an analogy to the syntax-manipulating function of a digital computer. A digital computer has for more than half a century been known to be able to outstrip the human capacity when it comes to (1) processing speed, (2) storage capacity and (3) processing accuracy. This is not some obscure ad hoc assumption conjured up to serve as footing for an anti-functionalist argument – it is an uncontroversial fact recognized even by elementary computer users. As a simple way of substantiating this claim, one may conduct the following informal tripartite tests, corresponding to the each of the three factors mentioned above. First, pick any simple, but computation intensive mathematical problems (like $879,284^{17} * 381,177^{31}$) and contrast the unaided human processing speed with that of a computer or a pocket calculator. Then, contrast the detailed encyclopedic knowledge of a single human being with that contained in the 32-volume Encyclopædia Britannica, and observe that a server installation easily boasts the capacity of storing that information a million times over. Finally, contrast the human accuracy in performing mathematical computations along with the detailed nature of human recall with that of the computer. Clearly and uncontroversially, as anyone can readily assess for himself, digital computers exceed human capacities when it comes to (1) processing speed, (2) storage capacity and (3) processing accuracy – and those are *the exact capacities that are exaggerated counterfactually by Searle's analogy* between the Chinese Room and a digital computer. Apart from processing speed, storage capacity and processing accuracy, the argument doesn't seem to require any other counterfactual assumptions,[38] and it thus merely makes counterfactual modifications to the human capacity that are fully coherent with the difference in human-machine capabilities that is already known to exist, in accordance with the overarching purpose of highlighting the in-principle deficiency suffered by a closed and ungrounded syntactical system.

Again, this by no means amounts to a defense of the Chinese Room Argument against a *general* deflationist attack on the epistemic force of thought experiments as such; rather, I think it shows that if one does grant some measure of epistemic force to thought experiments in philosophy, then the specific nature of the counterfactuality relied on in the Chinese Room Argument seems to tip the balance considerably in Searle's favor, on the question of the usefulness of his famous Gedankenexperiment.

References

Beenfeldt, C. (2005). "The Turing Test: Its Nature and Mentalistic Ontology." *The Danish Yearbook of Philosophy*, vol. 40. Museum Tusculanum Press.
Block, N. (2002). "Searle's Arguments against Cognitive Science. Views Into the Chinese Room," in Preston and Bishop (eds.). Oxford University Press.
Copeland, J. B. (2002). "The Chinese Room from a Logical Point of View. Views Into the Chinese Room," in Preston and Bishop (eds.). Oxford University Press.
Dennett, D. C. (1991). *Consciousness Explained*. Back Bay Books. Little, Brown and Company.
Dietrich, E. (1990). "Computationalism." *Social Epistemology*, 4.
Harnad, S. (1989). "Minds, Machines and Searle." *Journal of Theoretical and Experimental Artificial Intelligence*, 1.
Harnad, S. (1990). "The Symbol Grounding Problem." *Physica D*, 42.

Harnad, S. (1993). "Grounding Symbols in the Analog World with Neural Nets – A Hybrid model." *Think*, 2.

Harnad, S. (1994a). "Does Mind Piggyback on Robotic and Symbolic Capacity? The Mind, the Brain, and Complex Adaptive Systems," in Morowitz and Singer (eds.). Santa Fe Institute Studies in Complexity, XXII.

Harnad, S. (1994b). "Computation Is Just Interpretable Symbol Manipulation: Cognition Isn't." *Minds and Machines*, 4.

Harnad, S. (1994c). "Levels of Functional Equivalence in Reverse Bioengineering: The Darwinian Turing Test for Artificial Life." *Artificial Life*, 1.

Harnad, S. (1995). "Grounding Symbolic Capacity in Robotic Capacity. The 'artificial life' route to 'artificial intelligence': Building Situated Embodied Agents," in Steels and Brooks (eds.). New Haven: Lawrence Erlbaum.

Harnad, S. (2000). "Minds, Machines and Turing: The Indistinguishability of Indistinguishables." *Journal of Logic, Language, and Information* (Special Issue on Alan Turing), 9.

Harnad, S. (2002). "Minds, Machines, and Searle 2: What's Right and Wrong about the Chinese Room Argument. Views Into the Chinese Room," in Preston and Bishop (eds.). Oxford University Press.

Harre, R. and H. T. Wang (1999). "Setting up a real "Chinese Room": an empirical replication of a famous thought experiment." *Journal of Experimental and Theoretical Artificial Intelligence*, 11.

Haugeland, J. (2002). "Syntax, Semantics, Physics. Views Into the Chinese Room" (Preston and Bishop eds.). Oxford University Press.

Hauser, L. (1993). "Reaping the Whirlwind: Reply to Harnad's 'Other Bodies, Other Minds.'" *Minds and Machines*, 3.

Hodges, A. (1992). *Alan Turing: The Enigma*. Vintage publication.

Leiber, J. (1995). *On Turing's Turing Test and why the matter matters*. Syntese, 104.

McDermott, D. (1982). "Minds, brains, programs, and persons." *The Behavioral and Brain Sciences*, 5.

Morris, C. (1970) (originally published in 1938). *Fundations of the Theory of Signs*. University of Chicago Press.

Preson, J. (2002). "Introduction. Views Into the Chinese Room," in Preston and Bishop (eds.). Oxford University Press.

Preston, J. and Bishop, M. (eds.). (2002). *Views Into the Chinese Room*. Oxford University Press.

Searle, J. R. (1980). "Minds, Brains, and Programs." *The Behavioral and Brain Sciences*, 3.

Searle, J. R. (1982). "The Myth of the Computer." *New York Review of Books*, April 19.

Searle, J. R. (1989a). *Minds, Brains and Science. The 1984 Reith Lectures*. Penguin Books. Penguin Books.

Searle, J. R. (1989b). "Reply to Jacquette." *Philosophy and Phenomenological Research*, XLIX.

Searle, J. R. (1990a). "Is the Brain a Digital Computer?" *Proceedings and Addresses of the American Philosophical Association*, 64.

Searle, J. R. (1990b). "Is the Brain's Mind a Computer Program?" *Scientific American*, 262.

Searle, J. R. (1994). *The Rediscovery of the Mind*. MIT Press.

Searle, J. R. (1997). *The Mystery of Consciousness*. A New York Review of Books publication.

Searle, J. R. (2001). *A Companion to the Philosophy of Mind*, in Guttenplan (ed.). Blackwell Companions to Philosophy.

Searle, J. R. (2002). "Twenty-One Years in the Chinese Room. Views Into the Chinese Room," in Preston and Bishop (eds.). Oxford University Press.

Sun, R. (2000). "Symbol grounding: A new look at an old idea." *Philosophical Psychology*, 13.

Teng, N. (2000). "A cognitive analysis of the Chinese room argument." *Philosophical Psychology*, 13.

Turing, A. M. (1950). "Computing Machinery and Intelligence." *Mind: A Quarterly Review of Psychology and Philosophy*, LIX.

Notes

1. Searle 1980.
2. See Searle 2002 for John Searle's own recent discussion of the argument. Also, consult the 10-page bibliography of relevant works pertaining to the discussion of the argument in Preston and Bishop 2002
3. Preston 2002 (p. 2).
4. Dietrich 1994 (p. 5).
5. Teng 2000 (p. 316).
6. See Searle 2002 (pp. 51-5) and Harnad 2002 (p. 297) on the close connection between Strong AI and the Turing Test.
7. Searle 1989a (p. 32).
8. Searle 1989a (p. 31-4), 1994 (p. 45) and 1997 (pp. 10-3).
9. A test for determining whether computers can think, introduced by Alan Turing in the mid 20th century. The basic idea of the test is that the computers can think when we generally can't tell them apart from human beings after 5 minutes of text-based 'conversation'. See Turing 1950.
10. Searle 1990b (p. 20) and 1994 (p. 200).
11. Searle relies upon Morris' basic syntax/semantics distinction, but otherwise adopts a markedly different position from that of Morris. Specifically, Searle's view that syntax is not intrinsic to the physics of the system, i.e. is observer-relative, departs radically from Morris' view that anything, including natural a phenomenon like thunder, can function as a sign. See Morris 1970 (p. 12), Searle 1990a, 1997 (pp. 13-8) and 2002.
12. Morris 1970 (chapter III).
13. Morris 1970 (chapter IV).
14. Morris 1970 (chapter V).
15. Harnad 1994a (pp. 6-8). See also Harnad 1989, 1990, 1993 (pp. 3-4), 1994a (pp. 6-8), 1994b (pp. 6-7), 1994c, 1995 and 2000. Furthermore, see Sun 2000.
16. A symbol system is a set of physical tokens, manipulated on the basis of explicit rules exclusively according to the physical characteristics of the symbols, not on their intentional content or meaning.
17. See Beenfeldt 2005.
18. Searle 1982, 1989b and 2001.
19. Dennett 1991 (p. 439).
20. "It was the system as a whole that 'thought', in [Turing's] view, and it was its logical structure, not its particular physical embodiment that made this possible." Hodges 1992 (p. 405).
21. Copeland 2002 (p.174).
22. While this move mostly has been overlooked in the general Chinese Room Argument literature, it is nevertheless worth exploring a bit, since – as I will argue later in this paper – some of the lessons learned here will find application to later, and much more prominent, parts of the debate.
23. Hauser 1993 (p. 9).

24. Block 2002.
25. Haugeland 2002.
26. McDermott 1982.
27. McDermott 1982.
28. Block 2002 (p. 73).
29. McDermott 1982 (p. 340).
30. McDermott 1982 (p. 340).
31. McDermott 1982 (p. 340).
32. Block 2002 (p. 74).
33. Block 2002 (p. 74).
34. Block 2002 (p. 74).
35. This, of course, were what Turing and the other cryptologists at Bletchley Park used to break the German Enigma encryption. See Hodges 1992.
36. Leiber (1995).
37. Although a successful small-scale replication of the room mechanics has actually been made. See Harre and Wang 1999.
38. Of course, the programming ("rule writing") of the Chinese Room has to be good as well. It has to be as good as the first artificial intelligence program that wins the Loebner Prize.

GENEALOGIES OF MODERN TECHNOLOGY

SØREN RIIS

Roskilde University

Introduction

Does modern technology differ from ancient technology and does it have a unique essence? This twofold question opens one of Martin Heidegger's most influential philosophical inquiries, *The Question Concerning Technology*. The answer Heidegger offers has inspired various critiques and appraisals from a vast number of contemporary scholars of technology.[1] Heidegger's answer is traditionally thought to suggest a great difference between ancient and modern technology. However, by re-examining Heidegger's text, it is possible to discover previously ignored or misunderstood lines of thoughts that affirm a multi-stable interpretation of the origin of modern technology. In what follows, we shall see how *The Question Concerning Technology* in fact supports three different genealogies of modern technology. The guiding thought of our investigation is the following passage, where Heidegger relativises the manifestations of modern technology

> All coming to presence, not only modern technology, keeps itself everywhere concealed to the last. Nevertheless, it remains, with respect to its holding sway, that which precedes all: the earliest. The Greek thinkers already knew of this when they said: That which is earlier with regard to its rise into dominance becomes manifest to us men only later. That which is primarily early shows itself only ultimately to men. Therefore, in the realm of thinking, a painstaking effort to think through still more primally what was primally thought is not the absurd wish to revive what is past, but rather the sober readiness to be astounded before the coming of the dawn (Heidegger 1977a, p. 327).

We now want to take this 'painstaking effort' seriously, which Heidegger calls upon, and try 'to think still more primally' the origin of modern technology. As Heidegger points out, this may imply reversing commonly held understandings, for the 'origin' does often not show itself until the end.

I. The Modern Origin of Modern Technology

To be able to follow the line of thought presented in this paper and to see through the different layers of Heidegger's argument concerning the origin of the essence of modern technology, it is necessary to understand Heidegger's specific use of the concept of essence. Heidegger's point of departure is the antique understanding of essence:

> Technology is not equivalent to the essence of technology. When we are seeking the essence of "tree," we have to become aware that what pervades every tree, is not itself a tree that can be encountered among all the other trees. Likewise, the essence of technology is by no means anything technological (Heidegger 1977a, p. 327).

According to Heidegger, we should not focus on technology itself in order to understand what it essentially is. Heidegger argues that we should instead direct our attention towards technology as a way of bringing-forth and revealing beings. Technology discloses distinctive beings of different sorts when it is set to work – when technology is, *as it is*, it brings out of concealment into unconcealment as Heidegger at one point describes it (Heidegger 1977a, p. 317). Following Heidegger's line of thought, the essence of technology is not a substance of some sort, but rather a specific process of bringing-forth beings. From this insight into the essence of technology, Heidegger is able to show a crucial connection to the ancient Greek understanding of truth, alêtheia, and thereby re-address the importance of his investigation.

> Bringing-forth brings out of concealment into unconcealment. Bringing-forth propriates only insofar as something concealed comes into unconcealment. This coming rests and moves freely within what we call revealing. The Greeks have the word alêtheia for revealing. The Romans translate this with *veritas*. We say "truth" and usually understand it as correctness of representation (Heidegger 1977a, p. 317ff).

In order to be able to judge if a representation is 'correct', it is necessary that what is 're-presented' at first become 'present', which means 'unconcealed' in Heidegger's terminology. The Greek understanding of truth, which Heidegger brings to attention, is therefore primary to 'truth as correctness of representation'. It is in this fundamental sense of truth that Heidegger can conclude that technology is at way truth happens (Heidegger 1977a, p. 319ff). "But where have we strayed to? We are questioning concerning technology, and we have arrived now at alêtheia, at revealing. What has the essence of technology to do with revealing? The answer: everything. For every bringing-forth is grounded in revealing" (Heidegger 1977a, p. 318).

Before we take a closer look at Heidegger's investigation of the specific essence of modern technology and try to study its origin, that is the beginning of and the way in which modern technology brings-forth and thereby occasions truth, it is important to recognize the philosophical significance of Heidegger's approach. By connecting the essence of technology with the foundation of truth and ontology, Heidegger makes the understanding of technology indispensable to philosophical reflection. He thus is accredited as one of the founding fathers of philosophy of technology as he unfolds technology in a discourse of fundamental importance to philosophy.[2] The reason why Heidegger's philosophy of technology is studied with increasing interest and concern today does to a great extent rely on what we are about to examine – that is, Heidegger's challenging answer to the two more specific question: How does the world appear when revealed through modern technology and when did this revealing initially happen?

The essence of technology is to reveal beings, but according to Heidegger modern technology does so in a particular manner. In revealing beings, the essence of modern technology prepares nature to stand at command and be able to deliver what is ordered from it (Heidegger 1977a, p. 320). "The revealing that rules in modern technology is a challenging, which puts to nature the unreasonable demand that it supply energy which can be extracted and stored as such" (Heidegger 1977a, p. 320). The demand for energy is crucial to understand Heidegger's investigation of the challenging revealing of modern technology. His main example of the challenging revealing of modern technology – how modern technology essentially works – is a hydroelectric plant.

> The hydroelectric plant is set into the current of the Rhine. It sets the Rhine to supplying its hydraulic pressure, which then sets the turbines turning. This turning sets those machines in motion whose thrust sets going the electric current for which the long distance power station and its network of cables are set up to dispatch electricity. In the context of the interlocking processes pertaining to the orderly disposition of electrical energy, even the Rhine itself appears to be something at our command (Heidegger 1977a, p. 321).

The Rhine as revealed through modern technology appears as an energy resource, which stands at human disposal. Ultimately, through modern technology, nature in general is revealed as what Heidegger calls 'standing-reserve'. In order not to misunderstand this neologism, the concept of standing should not be associated with something inflexible or static. Nature revealed as a 'standing-reserve' is not at all static, it is mobilised and ready; it is prepared and now 'stands' under command. Heidegger therefore terms the essence of modern technology *das Ge-stell*, because he wants to stress this feature of the essence of modern technology (Heidegger 1977a, p. 324ff).[3] That this characteristic of *das Gestell* is crucial becomes increasingly clear when Heidegger explains the processes belonging to the challenging revealing of modern technology.

> Such challenging happens in that the energy concealed in nature is unlocked, what is unlocked is transformed, what is transformed is stored up, what is stored up is in turn distributed, and what is distributed is switched about ever anew. Unlocking, transforming, storing, distributing, and switching about are ways of revealing (Heidegger 1977a, p. 322).

The important link between the challenging revealing of modern technology and the production and control of energy and Heidegger's focus on the hydroelectric plant suggests that the origin of *das Gestell* is connected to modernity and the rise of electric energy. Heidegger's additional examples of modern technology in *The Question Concerning Technology* such as the airplane, the steam turbine and the cyclotron indeed further supports that Heidegger interprets the challenging revealing of modern technology, its essence, as a specific modern phenomenon (Heidegger 1977a, p. 322ff). In other words, Heidegger's text supports the majority of scholars, who interpret *The Question Concerning Technology* as Heidegger's polemic against modernity and connects the origin of *das Gestell* with the rise of modern technology and events taking place no earlier than the Industrial Revolution of the 18th and 19th century. Not least because of the great changes following the Industrial Revolution, this account of the location in history of the rise of the essence of modern technology has a great suggestive force. But what if Heidegger's examples were only the most clear-cut showcases of the rule of *das Gestell,* and its rule in fact preceded Heidegger's examples of the actual manifestations of modern technology? What if the *The Question Concerning Technology* in fact allows a 'more primal' interpretation of the origin of the essence of modern technology?

II. The Antique Origin of Modern Technology

If we read *The Question Concerning Technology* more closely, we come upon two passages which offer support to questioning the first account of the origin of modern technology. As we have seen, Heidegger describes the rule of *das Gestell* as putting the demand on nature to supply energy, and he illustrates this by way of a hydroelectric power plant. This description connects the rise of the essence of technology to the production of electrical energy and therefore suggests the origin of *das Gestell* no earlier than the 19th century and Michael Faraday's invention of the electric motor (see Morus 2004). From this perspective, the essence of modern technology arises in late modernity, and it is this genealogy we have outlined above. However, we must question this traditional account. Heidegger might want to connect the rule of *das Gestell* to late modernity, but in his analysis of the power of *das Gestell*, we find reasons to re-examine Heidegger's notion of energy, go beyond the rise of electric energy and locate the origin of the power of *das Gestell* before the events leading up to the production and organisation of electrical energy. The challenging revealing of nature belonging to the rule of *das Gestell* does, as we shall see in this second genealogy, not necessarily have to do with electricity; in fact Heidegger's own explanation implies a broader concept of standing-reserve than that of electric energy.

> In contrast, a tract of land is challenged in the hauling out of coal and ore, the earth now reveals itself as a coal mining district, the soil as a mineral deposit. The field that the peasant formerly cultivated and set in order appears differently than it did when to set it in order still meant to take care of and maintain... But meanwhile even the cultivation of the field has come under the grip of another kind of setting-in-order, which *sets upon* nature. It sets upon it in the sense of challenging it. Agriculture is now mechanized food industry. Air is now set upon to yield nitrogen, the earth to yield uranium, for example; uranium is set upon to yield atomic energy, which can be unleashed either for destructive or for peaceful purposes (Heidegger 1977a, p. 320).

Whereas coalmining and uranium production also relate to the 19th and 20th century and therefore to late modernity, Heidegger expresses in this passage a different meaning of the revealing of nature as energy namely as standing-reserve. According to this notion energy as standing-reserve also covers coal, ore and nitrogen as systematically used resources. It is exactly this kind of revealing of nature, which also has made the systematic use of wood, peat and turf available for centuries. In other words, analysing Heidegger's example, we can translate the notion of energy and standing-reserve to anything that is systematically used as a resource. Through this interpretation, we all of a sudden are allowed to assess the origin of the rule of *das Gestell* far beyond late modernity. In other words, to interpret standing-reserve as electrical energy makes some feature of the rule of *das Gestell* very intuitive, but to equal the two would be a too narrow interpretation, which the text rejects.

In another passage, which serves as our guideline for the whole inquiry presented in this paper, Heidegger argues in favour of reversing historical events in the light of their systematic origin. Heidegger suggests that we have to go past the appearance of modern technologies to understand the origin of their essence.

> But, after all, mathematical science arose almost two centuries before technology. How, then, could it have already been set upon by modern technology and placed in its service? The facts testify to the contrary. Surely technology got under way only when it could be supported by exact physical science. Reckoned chronologically, this is correct. Thought historically, it does not hit upon the truth (Heidegger 1977a, p. 326ff).

According to Heidegger's argument, modern technology is not applied science. Even though actual modern technology often relies on specific scientific insights, and the Scientific Revolution dates before the Industrial Revolution, Heidegger maintains that science is in fact based on the essence of technology, i.e. the world revealed as standing-resource. Heidegger notes that science, even as pure theory, "entraps nature as a calculable coherence of forces", which through experiment is ordered to give correct, reliable answers (Heidegger 1977a, p. 326).[4] Heidegger maintains that the framing of the nature belonging to modern mathematical science is dependent upon the exact world-disclosure, which is defined by *das Gestell*.

At first glance, Heidegger's argument in favour of the modern rise of a particular essence of modern technology has a great suggestive force as it seems to be supported by the great changes brought about by the Industrial Revolution. The changes in society and human behaviour taking place alongside modern industrial technology are precisely so thorough that many historians in fact agree to speak of a "revolution". This means that the Industrial Revolution is understood as a pivotal event: the world before the industrial technology is radically different from the world afterwards, and this would support the first genealogy of *das Gestell*. However, it is exactly the revolutionary aspect of the events taking place due to the rise of modern industrialised technology that Heidegger questions by saying that the essential changes took place long before – even before the Scientific Revolution happening approximately two centuries earlier in the 16th and 17th centuries (Heidegger, 1977a: 326f). Heidegger therefore seems to be saying that there were no real Scientific and Industrial Revolution – or, articulated more precisely: that these were only minor events and owed their unfolding to a much earlier and more groundbreaking event, namely the rise of the rule of *das Gestell*.[5] But when and how did *das Gestell* then rise to dominance according to *The Question Concerning Technology*? When did human beings start to view nature as a resource that could be transformed, transported and used?

If we take a closer look at Heidegger's understanding of ancient Greek technology and the way in which he describes the manufacturing of a silver chalice in *The Question Concerning Technology*, then we arrive at crucial results.

> Silver is that out of which the silver chalice is made. As this matter (*hyle*), it is co-responsible for the chalice. The chalice is indebted to, i.e., owes thanks to, the silver for that of which it consists. But the sacrificial vessel is indebted not only to the silver. As a chalice, that which is indebted to the silver appears in the aspect of a chalice, and not in that of a brooch or a ring. Thus the sacred vessel is at the same time indebted to the aspect (*eidos*) of the chaliceness. Both the silver into which the aspect is admitted as chalice and the aspect in which the silver appears are in their respective ways co-responsible for the sacrificial vessel (Heidegger 1977a, p. 315).

And Heidegger continues his description:

> But there remains yet a third something that is above all responsible for the sacrificial vessel. It is that which in advance confines the chalice within the realm of consecration and bestowal... That which gives bounds, that which completes, in this sense is called in Greek *telos*, which is all too often translated as "aim" and "purpose," and so misinterpreted. The *telos* is responsible for what as matter and what as aspect are together co-responsible for the sacrificial vessel... The silversmith considers carefully and gathers together the three aforementioned ways of being responsible and indebted... The silversmith is co-responsible as that from which the sacred vessel's being brought forth and subsistence take and retain their first departure (Heidegger 1977a, p. 315).

In order to be able to produce the chalice the silversmith must in advance imagine the aspect (*eidos*) of a chalice and afterwards shape the silver accordingly. The silversmith brings the aspect into being by way of the silver and his tools. The unspoken premise for this to happen it that nature can be dug out for ore, which can be melted, separated into components (silver and lead in this case) and additionally refined. After the ancient technology of mining has done its work, then the silversmith forces the shape of a chalice upon the silver by way of heating, hammering and engraving the silver. In other words, and as differentiated from the automatic bringing-forth belonging to nature, Heidegger writes: "In contrast, what is brought forth by the artisan or the artist, e.g., the silver chalice, has the irruption belonging to bringing-forth, *not in itself, but in another* (en allôi), *in the craftsman or artist* (Heidegger 1977a, p. 317; my emphasis)." That which the craftsman brings-forth does not take place by itself, rather he forces or in fact 'challenges' the silver to take on the aspect of a chalice – in order to correspond to the *eidos* he is imagining. We therefore understand 'challenge' in its fundamental meaning, namely as describing a process that does not happen by itself, but is artificially provoked or induced – a process which does not follow naturally from a thing itself and therefore does not belong to its essence.

As a connected course of events, the ancient technology of mining and manufacturing puts the demand on nature to deliver artefacts. Accordingly, Heidegger is right that ancient technology does not put the demand on nature to deliver energy in its modern sense, but instead ancient technology demands artefacts from nature. However, as we have seen, Heidegger's use of the concept "energy" does in fact not only mean electric energy, but also resources of a different kind, i.e. utensils such as a sacrificial vessel of silver. Therefore, the demand of ancient technology on nature to deliver artefacts challenges nature in the exact same substantial way as modern technology. We are therefore allowed to argue in favour of an ancient origin of the rule of *das Gestell*.

It is worth noticing that Heidegger's example concerning the 'silver chalice' is very wisely chosen, because it is difficult to say whether it is an artwork or a tool. Thereby, without really paying attention to it, we may enter a different discussion, and that is on the distinction between artworks and modern technology, and afterwards use a possible difference between these two domains in support of a difference between ancient and modern technology.[6] Therefore, we should direct our attention towards other products of ancient technology instead such as chairs, tables and weapons, which also count as technologies. Then we will see that ancient technology demands nature, trees and ore to deliver utensils and tools that stand ready, whenever needed. And exactly the same can be said about modern technology, as it for example also demands nature to deliver tables, chairs and weapons. By way of this argument we do not want to assert that there is no difference between ancient and modern technology, only that Heidegger's way of distinguishing the two does not hold up.

In fact, if we read other writings of Heidegger, we discover that Heidegger has another account of antiquity and modernity than the one which comes to the fore in *The Question Concerning Technology*, which radically separates the two epochs. In this other account, Heidegger argues that the modern understanding of and relation to nature is the completion of the antique conception of nature. That is to say, in this version of history Heidegger stresses that nature is considered malleable and is seen as a resource even in antiquity: With sufficient knowledge of the materials and the right sort of tools, the ancient craftsman could make nature a resource for all sorts of artefacts. Seen from this perspective, modernity is only the perfection of this antique beginning, and is basically dependent on the same revealing and framing of nature. This history Heidegger calls the history of metaphysics, and it manifests itself in the "interpretation of beings which brings their makeability to the fore" (Heidegger 1999, p. 88). In other words, and from a metaphysical point of view, ancient and modern technology rely on the same foundation and conception of being. Heidegger also writes: "It is very difficult to grasp historically the emergence of what is machinationally ownmost to beings, because basically it has been effectively since the first beginning of Western thinking" (Heidegger 1999, p. 92). In other words, the history of metaphysics and the understanding of the makeability of being ('machination') may be interpreted as Heidegger's explicit attempt to think the genealogy of *das Gestell* more primally and in connection to what Heidegger calls the 'first beginning' in Greek antiquity. As such, we read Heidegger's understanding of metaphysics as a consequence of what we took to be one of Heidegger's main thoughts in *The Question Concerning Technology*: "That which is primarily early shows itself only ultimately to men. Therefore, in the realm of thinking, a painstaking effort to think through still more primally what was primally thought is not the absurd wish to revive what is past, but rather the sober readiness to be astounded before the coming of the dawn" (Heidegger 1977, p. 327).

We do not want to venture further into Heidegger's understanding of metaphysics, as this would lead us away from our initial aim of showing three different genealogies of the modern technology and the rule of *das Gestell*. We have now already seen, from two different points of view, that antique and modern technology both rely on the same challenging understanding of nature according to which nature is framed in such a way that it is possible to use it as a resource. From the latter of these two perspectives Heidegger explicitly says that the fundamental challenging understanding of nature which allows the transformation of natural resources into utensils and artefacts has in fact been effectively present since antiquity (Heidegger 1999, p. 92). In other words, according to the second genealogy of *das Gestell*, Heidegger sees the beginning of its dominance already in antiquity and not first on the verge of modernity.

III. The Prehistoric Origin of Modern Technology

In *The Question Concerning Technology* there are elements of yet another account of the origin of the challenging revealing of nature, which we have seen Heidegger ascribe to the rule of *das Gestell*. This version of the genealogy of *das Gestell* appears only very marginalised in the text, but still in such a way that an important part of Heidegger's argument makes no sense without asserting this third genealogy. To be able to understand this third genealogy more clearly, we will also need to refer to Heidegger's main work *Being and Time*.

The passage in *The Question Concerning Technology*, which calls on our attention and can help us discovering a third genealogy of *das Gestell* is the following.

> Where and how does this revealing happen if it is no mere handiwork of man? We need not look far. We need only apprehend in an unbiased way that which has already claimed man so decisively that he can only be man at any given time as the one so claimed. Wherever man opens his eyes and ears, unlocks his heart, and gives himself over to meditation and striving, shaping and working, entreating and thanking, he finds himself *everywhere already* brought into the unconcealed (Heidegger 1977a, p. 327; my emphasis).

Here Heidegger argues in favour of a primary revealing of nature, which takes place even before the "shaping and working" belonging to ancient technology, which we have studied above. But how are we to understand this fundamental kind of revealing? Let us first see a parallel line of thought from another lecture, where Heidegger unfolds the same phenomenology of the world, before we try to go further into Heidegger's argument.

> We never really first perceive a throng of sensations, e.g., tones and noises, in the appearance of things...; rather we hear the storm whistling in the chimney, we hear the three-motored plane, we hear the Mercedes in immediate distinction from the Volkswagen. Much closer to us than all sensations are the things themselves. We hear the door shut in the house and never hear acoustical sensations or even mere sounds. In order to hear a bare sound we have to listen away from things, divert our ear from them, i.e., listen abstractly (Heidegger 1977b, p. 151f).

The comprehensive theory behind these two passages is unfolded in *Being and Time*. The reason why Heidegger can assert that humans are '*everywhere already* brought into the unconcealed' and 'much closer to us than all sensations are the things themselves' is due to Heidegger's fundamental understanding of how humans are in the world. According to Heidegger, humans do not live in some sort of isolation from where they have to get out in order to maintain a relation to the things around them (Heidegger 1962, p. 78ff). Humans live undetachable from the world, nature is always already revealed to them and it is this specific unconcealment, which Heidegger elaborates in *Being and Time*.

> In equipment that is used, 'Nature' is discovered along with it by that use – the 'Nature' we find in natural products.
> Here, however, 'Nature' is not to be understood as that which is just present-at-hand, nor as the *power of Nature*. The wood is a forest of timber, the mountain a quarry of rock; the river is waterpower, the wind is wind 'in the sails' (Heidegger 1962, p. 100).

This explanation throws new light on *The Question Concerning Technology*, where Heidegger explains the challenging revealing of nature, which characterises *das Gestell* and becomes manifest in the mining of land for coal and ore and the use of the river for water power (Heidegger, 1977a: 320f). In other words, the challenging revealing of nature belonging to *das Gestell*, viewed through the optics of *Time and Being*, is not a modern phenomenon, but is as old as mankind. According to Heidegger's theory in *Being and Time*, everything in nature is always already unconcealed on the background of an instrumental context – things in nature appear seemingly unmediated 'in-order-to' and 'ready-to-hand' as Heidegger points out (Heidegger 1962, p. 105ff). And this instrumental framework that challenges everything to reveal itself as an instrument, is according to Heidegger the very condition for anything to be meaningful: To have a meaning entails to be revealed in a network of resources.

> We have indicated that the state which is constitutive for the ready-to-hand as equipment is one of reference or assignment... As definite kinds of references we have mentioned serviceability-for-, detrimentality, usability, and the like. The 'towards-which' of a serviceability and the 'for-which' of a usability prescribed the ways in which such a reference or assignment can become concrete... *An entity is discovered* [revealed] *when it has been assigned or referred to something*, and referred as that entity which it is. *With* any such entity there is an involvement [Bewandtnis] which it has *in* something. The character of Being which belongs to the ready-to-hand is just such an involvement (Heidegger 1962, p. 114f; my emphasis).

In addition, Heidegger also maintains: "*Readiness-to-hand is the way in which entities as they are 'in themselves' are defined ontologico-categorially*" (Heidegger 1962, p. 101).[7] According to Heidegger's fundamental phenomenology, which he unfolds in detail in *Being and Time* and reaffirms a crucial part of in *The Question Concerning Technology*, nature is 'primally' revealed in its 'serviceability' and 'usability' – that is to say, nature appears as a resource long before the rise of modern technology, namely simultaneously with the very origin of human beings.

Based on a decisive passage in *The Question Concerning Technology* and completed through references to *Being and Time* we finally have a genealogy of the essence of modern technology, which traces back the rule of *das Gestell* to the beginning of humankind. This is not to say that prehistoric technology is identical to modern technology; much rather the third genealogy suggests that when 'we still more primally' try to consider the beginning of the challenging revealing of *das Gestell*, then we in fact rediscover it as connected to the origin of humankind. The rule of *das Gestell* has prevailed as long as humans have been living on earth if we follow Heidegger's line of thought. And by way of thinking the genealogy of *das Gestell* more primally we arrive at a much more comprehensive understanding of modern technology itself. Trying to understand the various genealogies more or less explicitly present in *The Question Concerning Technology* is not just an exercise, nor only a way to criticise Heidegger, but a means to better understand the nuances and layers in Heidegger's thinking concerning technology. On this background we will give the last word to Heidegger: "Origin here means that from which and by which something is what it is and as it is. What something is, as it is, we call its essence. The origin of something is the source of its essence" (Heidegger 1977b, p. 143).

References

Harman, G. (2002). *Tool-Being. Heidegger and the Metaphysics of Objects* (Chicago/La Salle, Open Court).
Heidegger, M. (1962). *Being and Time* (Oxford, Blackwell Publishers)
Heidegger, M. (1977a). "The Question Concerning Technology", in David Farrell Krell (ed.) *Basic Writings* (NY, Harper & Row).
Heidegger, M. (1977b). "The Origin of the Work of Art", in David Farrell Krell (ed.) *Basic Writings* (NY, Harper & Row).
Heidegger, M. (1999). *Contributions to Philosophy: From Enowning* (Bloomington, IN, Indiana University Press).
Ihde, Don (1979). *Technics and Praxis* (Dordrecht, D. Reidel Publishing Company).
Krieger, M. H. (1992). *Doing Physics: How Physicists Take Hold of the World* (Bloomington, IN, Indiana University Press).
Morus, Iwan R (2004). *Michael Faraday and the Electrical Century* (Cambridge, Icon Books).
Riis, S. (forthcoming) *Zur Neubestimmung der Technik: Eine Auseinandersetzung mit Martin Heidegger.*
Scharff, Robert C. and Val Dusek (2003). "Introduction to Part IV: Heidegger on Technology", in Robert C. Scharff and Val Dusek (eds.), *Philosophy of Technology: the technological Condition: an Anthology* (Oxford, Blackwell Publishing).
Shapin, Steven (1996). *The Scientific Revolution* (Chicago, The University of Chicago Press).

Notes

1. See also: "Most philosophers of technology would probably agree that, for good or ill, Martin Heidegger's interpretation of technology, its meaning in Western history, and its role in contemporary human affairs is probably the single most influential position in the field" (Scharff, R. C. and Val Dusek 2003, p. 247).
2. See Scharff, R. C. and Val Dusek 2003, p. 247.
3. Because the English translation of *das Gestell*, the enframing, does not refer to a specific 'stand', I shall continue to use the German concept 'Gestell' to characterize what Heidegger means by the essence of modern technology. Another translation of *das Gestell*, which would call attention to this feature, would be "set-up".
4. See also Krieger (1992).
5. Steven Shapin (1996) also argues against the revolutionary aspect of the 'Scientific Revolution': "There was no such thing as the Scientific Revolution, and this is a book about it. Some time ago, when the academic world offered more certainty and more comforts, historians announced the real existence of a coherent, cataclysmic, and climatic event that fundamentally and irrevocably changed what people knew about the natural world and how they secured proper knowledge of that world" (Shapin 1996, p. 1).
6. For a more elaborate account of this aspect see my forthcoming dissertation: Riis, S. *Zur Neubestimmung der Technik: Eine Auseinandersetzung mit Martin Heidegger.*
7. See as well: "The nature of the ready-to-hand does anticipate the notion of standing reserve." (Ihde, D. 1979, p. 124.) See also Graham Harman's description of the transition from ready-to-hand to present-at-hand: "In the first instance [ready-to-hand], every object is obliterated, withdrawing into its tool-being in the contexture of the world. In this way, the individual objects are smothered and *enslaved*, emerging into the sun only in the moment of their breakdown" (Harman, G. 2002, p. 45).

SKEPTICISM AND TRANSCENDENTAL ARGUMENTS FROM SEMANTIC EXTERNALISM

ESBEN NEDENSKOV PETERSEN
University of Southern Denmark

I. The Aim and Structure of Transcendental Arguments against External world Skepticism

It remains a matter of some dispute what it takes for an argument to be appropriately referred to as a transcendental argument, and whether so called transcendental arguments really deserve a predicate borrowing the term 'transcendental' from Kant's *Critique of Pure Reason*.[1] In the present paper, however, I allow myself to leave these disputes aside, since conventional usage of the predicate in epistemology appears to delineate a notion making it reasonably clear what subclass of arguments one is referring to when speaking of transcendental arguments against external world skepticism.

Accordingly, the arguments referred to as transcendental arguments against skepticism generally share the following structure (where 'p' abbreviates a proposition about the external world, which could not be known to be true according to a supposed skeptic):

(TA1) A relatively uncontroversial proposition, or relatively uncontroversial propositions, about the phenomenology of thought or experience.

(TA2) A further proposition, or further propositions, saying that the aforementioned propositions about the phenomenology of thought or experience entail the truth of *p*.

And,

(TA3) The conclusion that *p* is true.

Moreover, according to the proponents of transcendental arguments, the premises of such arguments can be known to be true a priori, that is, based solely on reflection and the phenomenology of experience. This means that transcendental arguments against skepticism are supposed to take us from knowledge of uncontroversial truths about thought and phenomenological experience to truths about the external world by employing a priori knowable principles "bridging the gap" between appearance and reality.

This shared structure of transcendental arguments owes to their being put forward with the shared aim of establishing the falsity of external world skepticism based on premises that are not threatened by the necessary conditions on knowledge proposed by the skeptic. In other words, by being taken to proceed from premises that the skeptic would accept as known despite of her conceptual vantage point, arguments of this kind are supposed to deliver something, which the skeptic herself might acknowledge as proof of the falsity of skepticism without relinquishing her assumptions about the necessary conditions on knowledge. Consequently, the aim of proponents of transcendental arguments imposes the significant restriction on this kind of argument that it has to reach its rejection of skepticism without relying on a conceptual analysis showing the skeptic to be mistaken about the concept of knowledge. Indeed, a transcendental argument could hardly be taken to proceed from premises that the skeptic might accept as known despite of her conceptual commitments if accepting the argument would require the skeptic to abandon her initial assumptions about the necessary conditions on knowledge.

Moreover, insofar as we take a rejection of skepticism subject to the above restrictions to be the aim of transcendental arguments, it follows that arguments of this kind, that is, arguments sharing the general logical structure outlined above, can only be used to target a particular range of skeptical positions. A global skepticism proposing necessary conditions on knowledge from which it follows that we do not know anything could not be targeted by transcendental arguments, because any argument against global skepticism would have to rely on premises, which cannot be known according to a global skeptic. For a transcendental argument with premises correspond to (TA1) and (TA2) to get of the ground some kind of foothold for the premises will be required. At least some propositions about the phenomenology of thought and experience have to be left untouched by the conditions on knowledge proposed by the skeptic to make her vulnerable to transcendental arguments. But on the other hand, if the entire range of propositions about how things appear in experience is left untouched by a skeptic, then any premise corresponding with (TA1) could be employed to prove the falsity of her particular version of skepticism. If this is the case, then any true proposition about experiential states of affairs will be available for the construction of a transcendental argument. And if any such proposition can be combined with an a priori knowable principle corresponding with (TA2) to form a transcendental argument, then inferring its conclusion from the premises will yield an instance of knowledge about the world beyond experience.[2]

Consequently, a transcendental argument relying on a plausible a priori principle to establish the falsity of the claim that I am a brain in vat would yield a strong objection to a skeptical argument like the following (letting 'e' abbreviate the proposition 'that the diachronic totality of my experiences ranges over the phenomenological appearances E'):

(SA)

(SA1) I can only know the truth of a proposition p if e entails that p is true.

(SA2) The truth of the proposition that I am not a brain in a vat is not entailed by e.

Hence,

(SA3) I do not know that I am not a brain in a vat.

And whereas the majority of analytical philosophers doing epistemology would respond to such a skeptical argument by arguing that we should reject (SA1) as a necessary condition on knowledge, a proponent of a transcendental argument against (SA) would argue that we could reject the skeptical conclusion based on premises undermining (SA2) while leaving (SA1) untouched.

This line against the skeptic is famously taken by P. F. Strawson in *Individuals* from 1959 and in *The Bounds of Sense* from 1966, where he endeavoured to reach a rebuttal of skepticism building on the considerations laid out by Kant in the Transcendental Deduction of the *Critique of Pure Reason*. But in his Woodbridge Lectures[3] from 1983, Strawson abandoned his initial strategy for rejecting skepticism in the light of objections put forward against the arguments of his earlier works,[4] and argued that the quest for such a rebuttal should be considered mistaken.[5]

However, not everyone has followed Strawson in thinking the pursuit of a transcendental argument against skepticism mistaken. Accordingly, the central discussion of this paper concerns the transcendental argument put forward by Anthony Brueckner in the 1993 article "Semantic Answers to Skepticism", where it is argued that skepticism of the above kind can be refuted by relying on a priori knowledge of the truth of semantic externalism.

For the purpose of this discussion, the following section of the paper outlines the basic tenets of semantic externalism and sets out the transcendental argument proposed by Brueckner. In the third section of the paper, I then present what I take to be the central objection against the argument. And I go on to demonstrate that the same objection applies to a similar argument put forward by Ted Warfield. Finally, the fourth section concludes the paper with some brief general remarks about semantic externalism and skepticism.

II. Semantic Externalism and the Transcendental Argument of Brueckner

That an anti-skeptical argument might be developed based on semantic externalism was first suggested by Putnam in his 1981 article "Brains in a Vat". What Putnam points out is that following semantic externalism the meaning of the words and sentences that enter into utterances and thoughts depend on states of affairs external to phenomenological experience. The reference of words and sentences, for example the reference of the terms 'tree', 'car', and 'boat', are thus said to be determined by causal connections linking together thoughts and utterances involving tokens of these terms with the things to which the terms refer. This means that in a world corresponding to the common sense view the term 'tree' refers to trees by being causally connected to trees in the external world in an appropriate way. Accordingly, thoughts involving tokens of the term 'tree' would not have any reference to trees, if one was a brain in a vat with experiences as of seeing trees in a world with no trees, because then the thoughts in question could not be causally connected to trees in the external world.

For someone who is actually a brain in vat being fed experiences controlled by a computer program this has the consequence that if she was to have the thought 'I am a brain in vat', then the tokens 'brain' and 'vat' included in her thought would not refer to a brain and a vat. That is, her thought would not have the appropriate causal connections to brains and vats, but would be causally connected to brains and vats "in the image, or to [...] electronic impulses [...], or to the features of the program that are responsible for those electronic impulses."[6] Hence, the thought 'I am a brain in a vat' would not have the same meaning as a token of the sentence in a world corresponding to the common sense view. Instead, it would have a meaning, which in the language of the common sense world would translate into something along the lines of 'I am a brain-in-the-image in a vat-in-the-image', or no meaning at all. But since being a brain in a vat is obviously very different from being a brain-in-the-image in a vat-in-the-image, an actual brain in a vat would clearly be thinking something false when having the thought 'I am a brain in a vat'. And since someone who is not a brain in a vat would likewise be having a false thought when thinking 'I am a brain in a vat', it follows that it is necessarily false to think this thought.

But although the above may sound like a refutation of (SA2), it is not. To refute the skeptic by rejecting (SA2) the anti-skeptic has to establish not only that one could not truthfully think of oneself that one is a brain in a vat, but also that one could not *be* a brain in a vat. And doing this by way of a transcendental argument based on semantic externalism requires more than the above considerations deliver.

Nonetheless, Anthony Brueckner proposes that semantic externalism might be taken to provide a foundation for developing a transcendental argument refuting (SH).

The starting point of the argument set out by Brueckner is the claim that an essential feature of semantic externalism is that it has the consequence that (with the term 'BIV' abbreviating 'brain in a vat):

(EX) Necessarily, for all x, if x is a BIV, then x's thought 'I am a BIV' is true iff x is a BIV*.

Where 'x is a BIV*' represents what Brueckner refers to as the non-disquotational Putnamian truth conditions of the token thought *'I am a BIV'*, whatever they are in a particular case.

Consequently, understanding what Brueckner means by (EX) requires an understanding of what he means when speaking of sentences with non-disquotational truth conditions. This can best be explained on the background of his definition of sentences with disquotational truth conditions.

What he says about sentences with disquotational truth conditions is that they do not have disquotational truth conditions in themselves, but relative to a metalanguage ML, such that a token sentence S expressed in the object language L has disquotational truth conditions relative to a metalanguage ML iff,

"S' is true in L iff S', forms a true sentence in ML when the term 'is true in L iff' is translated into ML.

With this definition of disquotational truth conditions in place, Brueckner simplifies his presentation by speaking of token sentences as having disquotational truth conditions whenever the token sentences have disquotational truth conditions relative to his language, while speaking of token sentences as having non-disquotational truth conditions whenever they have non-disquotational truth conditions relative to his language. However, to simplify things in a similar way in the presentation of the argument here, I will henceforth say of a token sentence that it has non-disquotational truth conditions when it has non-disquotational truth conditions relative to my language, and that it has disquotational truth conditions when it has disquotational truth conditions relative to my language. And, in accordance with this, I will refer to my language as the metalanguage.

Thus, leaving in the specification 'relative to my language' to make things more clear, but otherwise following the terminology defined above, one should understand the above statement of (EX) as saying that:

(EX)   Necessarily, for all x, if x is a BIV, then x's thought 'I am a BIV' is true iff *particular truth conditions that are non-disquotational relative to my language are satisfied.*

In other words, according to Brueckner, it is necessarily true that my thought '*I am a BIV*' would not have the truth conditions I am a BIV if I was a BIV. In that case, my term 'BIV' would not refer to brains in vats, but to whatever has the appropriate causal connection with the term in my language. And, consequently, my thought '*I am a BIV*' would have truth conditions along the lines I am a brain-in-a-vat-in-the-image, if any.

Brueckner then argues that since the truth of propositions such as (EX) is an essential feature of semantic externalism, one could not be said to know the truth of semantic externalism without knowing the truth of propositions like (EX). And so it would appear that I could know the truth of (EX) a priori, since the truth of semantic externalism is supposed to be knowable a priori.

Moreover, if I know that (EX) holds, then I can know that the following strict conditional holds, since it is entailed by (EX):

(Cond) If I am a BIV, then my thought 'I am a BIV' is true iff I am a BIV*.

This means that in every possible world where I am a BIV the antecedent of the conditional (Cond) is true. And, consequently, I can know that in every possible world where I am a BIV it is true that:

(Cons) My thought 'I am a BIV' is true iff I am a BIV*.

But (Cons) could only be true of me in a world where I am envatted, if it is expressed by me in a world where I am not envatted, that is, if I am not envatted in the actual world. Thus, if I am envatted, the token sentence '*I am a BIV*' in the object language has a meaning identical to the meaning of the sentence '*I am BIV*' in the metalanguage. Accordingly, in the metalanguage, my language, which would then be the language of a BIV, the thought '*my thought 'I am a BIV' is true iff I am a BIV*' would then be true. And since this would imply that the sentence '*my thought 'I am a BIV' is true*' is disquotational, (Cons) would thereby be false.

According to Brueckner, however, I know the truth of the proposition expressed by (Cons) based on the inferences from (EX) and (Cond). So my use of the token sentence (Cons) must be a use of the term within the language of someone who is not a brain in a vat. And, hence, I can know that I am not a brain in a vat.

III. The Basic Problem with the Argument of Brueckner

Now, obviously, the skeptic could withstand this objection to (SA) by rejecting semantic externalism. For the purpose of the present discussion, however, I will not be questioning the merits of this view. According to Brueckner, this commits me to saying that (EX) can be known to be true, since conditionals like (EX) are constitutive of semantic externalism. And so, because the truth of semantic externalism is said to be knowable a priori, it follows that statements such as (EX), which are constitutive of semantic externalism, can also be known to hold a priori. But although this may be true, it does not provide adequate support for the argument put forward by Brueckner, since it does not allow him to state the anti-skeptical argument from semantic externalism based on premises, which are knowable according to (SA1).

The problem with the argument is that, since the semantic contents of thoughts and beliefs depend on states of affairs beyond phenomenology, the range of true propositions about the phenomenology of a subject having a thought with a particular semantic content does not entail that the thought in question has this particular content. Someone having a token thought with the propositional content expressed by (EX) in the language of an embodied person could have a phenomenology identical to the phenomenology of someone having a token thought with the propositional content expressed by (EX) in the language of a brain in a vat. So although semantic externalism implies that the proposition expressed by (EX) is necessarily true in the language of an embodied subject, I might thus fail to be semantically equipped in the way necessary for knowing this necessary truth, despite of having a phenomenology identical to that of someone who is thus equipped.

For this reason a subject making the inference from (EX) to (Cond) might come to know the truth of the proposition (Cond), but would not thereby come to know that she knows the truth of the proposition. Hence, for a subject to know whether she has made an inference from the proposition expressed by the token sentence (EX) in the language of an embodied subject or in the language of a brain in a vat, she would have to know beforehand whether she is an embodied subject or a brain in a vat. Someone making the inference from (Cond) to (Cons) might come to know that (Cons), but would not know whether she knows that (Cons), since she would not know whether she had made an inference from the proposition expressed by the token sentence (Cond) in the language of an embodied subject or in the language of a brain in a vat.

This raises a problem for Brueckner, since the conclusion of his argument does not follow from the mere truth of the proposition (Cons), which leaves open the possibility that I am a brain in vat unable to grasp the necessary truth of this proposition. Thus, in order to establish that the token sentence '*my thought 'I am a BIV' is true iff I am a BIV**' is not expressed in the language of an envatted brain, the argument of Brueckner requires the truth of the premise stating that the proposition expressed by the token sentence (Cons) is known to be true. But this premise could not be known to be true, according to our supposed skeptic since that would require knowing that the token sentence expresses the true proposition expressed by the token sentence (Cons) in the language of an embodied subject rather than the false proposition expressed by the token sentence (Cons) in the language of an envatted brain. Hence, the conclusion of the argument put forward by Brueckner follows from premises that could not be considered knowable by a skeptic claiming (SA1) to be a necessary condition on knowledge. And since the argument reaches its conclusion by relying on premises that are not knowable, according to (SA1), the soundness of the argument does not imply that a skeptic endorsing this claim should consider its conclusion knowable.

In other words, the claim that the truth of the propositions (EX), (Cond) and (Cons) can be known a priori, since knowledge of the propositions is constitutive of knowing the a priori truth of semantic externalism, can only be said to hold on the assumption that we are adequately equipped semantically to entertain the propositions expressed by the token sentences (EX), (Cond) and (Cons) in the language of an embodied subject. And since relying on this assumption amounts to assuming that we are not brains in vats, the assumption that one can know the truth of (EX), (Cond) and (Cons) could not be made without begging the question against the sceptical argument (SA) by assuming that (SA1) is false. Hence, if knowing the truth of these propositions is constitutive of knowing the truth of semantic externalism, and (SA1) is left unchallenged, then Brueckner will have to accept that the truth of semantic externalism can only be known by someone fortunate enough to be an embodied subject rather than a brain in a vat.

Moreover, this response to the argument of Brueckner can be applied in a very straightforward way to demonstrate that there is a parallel problem with a transcendental argument proposed by Ted Warfield. The argument put forward by Warfield takes the following form:

(TS1) I think that water is wet.

(TS2) No brain in a vat in an otherwise empty world can think that water is wet.

Hence,

(TS3) I am not a brain in a vat in an otherwise empty world.[7]

Here Warfield is depending on semantic externalism to establish (TS2). So for the sake of argument, let us keep in place the assumption that (TS2) is a priori knowable, while the supposed knowability of (TS1) simply relies on the assumption that we know the contents of our own thoughts, and therefore know that we have thoughts about water.

With this in place, what we get with the argument of Warfield is, basically, a version of the argument proposed by Brueckner, but stripped of technicalities. When considering our response to the argument of Brueckner it should, hence, be obvious that there is an identical problem concerning this parallel argument. Accordingly, the possibility of knowing that one knows (Cons) was rejected, because semantic externalism implies that although the semantic contents of their thoughts will be entirely dissimilar, an embodied subject with the token thought '*my thought 'I am a BIV' is true iff I am a BIV**' could have a phenomenology identical to the phenomenology of an envatted brain. And for much the same reason, there is a problem with (TS1), since it follows from (SA1) and semantic externalism that one could be thinking that water-in-the-image is wet instead of thinking that water is wet, without knowing whether one is thinking the former or the latter.

So the problem with the argument of Warfield is that, although (TS1) appears to be a proposition that the skeptic would consider knowable, the semantic externalism underlying (TS2) will make the claim that one could know (TS1) untenable to a skeptic arguing that the truth of everything I know must follow from how things appear to me in experience. And while it may seem obvious to some that we should object to considering this a necessary condition on knowledge, such a response to the skeptic is not available to someone aiming to refute skepticism on the basis of a transcendental argument. To challenge the necessary condition on knowledge proposed by the skeptic she would have to call upon a conceptual analysis, and an answer to skepticism resulting from such an analysis would obviously not yield an argument establishing the truth of propositions about the external world based on premises, which a skeptic would consider knowable.

IV. Concluding Remarks about Skepticism and Semantic Externalism

What then should we take with us from the preceding discussion? Well, an overall point appears to have emerged concerning the relation between semantic externalism and external world skepticism. A consequence of semantic externalism appears to be that claims about things considered strictly phenomenological in nature from a Cartesian point of view, such as the meaning of terms, the contents of thoughts, and so on, become vulnerable to skeptical doubts. Hence, in order to challenge the skeptic with a transcendental argument based on semantic externalism, without begging the question against her, one would have to demonstrate that the external factors determining the semantic content of our thoughts are such that one could not have a phenomenology identical to a subject thinking about brains without actually having thoughts about brains. And no principle involving this kind of necessary relation between appearance and reality follows from semantic externalism. Indeed, since no such principle appears to be forthcoming, a semantic externalist should take the preceding considerations to imply that some measure of conceptual analysis will be required by her, not just to claim that we know things about the external world, but also to uphold the assumption that we know the contents of our own thoughts.

References

Brueckner, Anthony (1994). "The Structure of the Skeptical Argument", *Philosophy and Phenomenological Research*, 54, pp. 827-835.

Brueckner, Anthony (1999a). "Semantic Answers to Skepticism", in DeRose, Keith & Warfield, Ted (eds.) *Skepticism: a Contemporary Reader* (Oxford, Oxford University Press).

Brueckner, Anthony (1999b). "Transcendental Arguments from Content Externalism", in Stern, Robert (ed.) *Transcendental Arguments* (Oxford, Oxford University Press).

DeRose, Keith & Warfield, Ted (eds.) (1999). *Skepticism: a Contemporary Reader* (Oxford, Oxford University Press).

Descartes, René (1996). *Meditations on First Philosophy* (New York, Cambridge University Press).

Hawthorne, John (2004). *Knowledge and Lotteries* (Oxford, Oxford University Press).

Hookway, Christopher (1999). Modest Transcendental Arguments and Sceptical Doubts, in Stern, Robert (ed.) *Transcendental Arguments* (Oxford, Oxford University Press), pp. 173-188.

Klausen, Søren Harnow (2004). *Reality Lost and Found* (Odense, University Press of Southern Denmark).

McCulloch, Gregory (1999). Content Externalism and Cartesian Scepticism: A Reply to Brueckner, in Stern, Robert (ed.) *Transcendental Arguments* (Oxford, Oxford University Press).

Pritchard, Duncan (2005). The Structure of Sceptical Arguments, *The Philosophical Quarterly*, 55, pp. 37-52.

Putnam, Hilary (1999). Brains in a Vat, in DeRose, Keith & Warfield, Ted (eds.), *Skepticism: a Contemporary Reader* (Oxford, Oxford University Press).

Stern, Robert (ed.) (1999a). *Transcendental Arguments* (Oxford, Oxford University Press).

Stern, Robert (1999b). "Introduction" in Stern, Robert (ed.) *Transcendental Arguments* (Oxford, Oxford University Press).

Strawson, Peter F. (1959). *Individuals* (London, Methuen).

Strawson, Peter F. (1966). *The Bounds of Sense* (London, Methuen).

Strawson, Peter F. (1985). *Skepticism and Naturalism: Some Varieties* (London, Methuen).

Stroud, Barry (1968). "Transcendental Arguments", *Journal of Philosophy*, 65, pp. 241-256.

Stroud, Barry (1984). *The Significance of Philosophical Scepticism* (Oxford, Oxford University Press).

Stroud, Barry (1999). "The Goal of Transcendental Arguments", in Stern, Robert (ed.) *Transcendental Arguments* (Oxford, Oxford University Press).

Vogel, Jonathan (2004). "Skeptical Arguments", *Philosophical Issues*, 14, pp. 426-455.

Warfield, Ted (1999). "A Priori Knowledge of the World: Knowing the World by Knowing Our Minds," in DeRose, Keith & Warfield, Ted (eds.) *Skepticism: a Contemporary Reader* (Oxford, Oxford University Press).

Notes

1. Klausen (2004) pp. 227-228.
2. This at least will be the case following the highly plausible principle of epistemic closure advocated by Timothy Williamson and John Hawthorne. See Hawthorne (2004) pp. 31-50.
3. Strawson (1985).
4. In particular, the objection put forward in Stroud (1968).
5. Indeed, he goes so far as to say that: "The correct way with the professional skeptical doubt is not to attempt to rebut it with argument, but to point out that it is idle, unreal, a pretense; and then the rebutting arguments will appear as equally idle..." Strawson (1983) p. 19. But while this is certainly and interesting change in view, I will not be discussing its merits in the present context.
6. Putnam (1999) p. 36.
7. Warfield (1999) p. 78.